ALSO BY BRUCE PANDOLFINI:

Let's Play Chess
Bobby Fischer's Outrageous Chess Moves
One Move Chess by the Champions
Principles of the New Chess

THE
ABCs
OF
CHESS

Invaluable, Detailed Lessons for Players at All Levels

---

by BRUCE PANDOLFINI

A FIRESIDE BOOK
Published by Simon & Schuster, Inc.
NEW YORK

A Fireside Book
Published by Simon & Schuster, Inc.
Simon & Schuster Building
Rockefeller Center
1230 Avenue of the Americas
New York, New York 10020

FIRESIDE and colophon are registered trademarks of Simon &
Schuster, Inc.

Designed by Stanley S. Drate/Folio Graphics Co. Inc.
Manufactured in the United States of America

10 9 8 7 6 5 4

Library of Congress Cataloging in Publication Data

Pandolfini, Bruce.
  The ABCs of chess.

  "A Fireside book."
  Originally appeared in various issues of Chess
life magazine.
  1. Chess. I. Title.
GV1445.P2578 1986   794.1'2   86-1831
ISBN: 0-671-61982-9

ACKNOWLEDGMENTS

My thanks to Idelle Pandolfini, Carol Ann Caronia, David Daniels, Paul Hoffmann, Deborah Bergman and Roane Carey.

For
Burt Hochberg,
Fairfield W. Hoban,
Frank Elley and Larry Parr

CONTENTS

About the ABCs

How to characterize a column that's evolved over a decade under four different editors—that's the question. So many changes have occurred in that period. Still, *Chess Life's* "ABCs of Chess" is what it always was: an innovative, introductory feature, clearly written, fully explanatory, and filled with concrete examples that illustrate the game's fundamentals. That it also scopes beyond this framework to break new ground in unveiling original instructional techniques is one of its distinctions.

Burt Hochberg, *Chess Life's* editor for thirteen years, sparked matters initially. He envisioned a column that would respond to the needs of the growing numbers of newcomers inspired to read the magazine in the aftermath of the Fischer-Spassky championship match of 1972, a column written primarily for players at a student level by experienced, professional chess teachers. Larry D. Evans, Julio Kaplan, and I were to write individually on the three phases of chess—Evans on the opening, Kaplan on the middlegame, and I on the endgame. All three of us were pleasantly surprised to discover that the columns would use the more convenient algebraic notation—then new to most Americans—in place of the more ambiguous descriptive notation.

Originally all three of us intended to write about the same game in one or more issues, but we immediately encountered obstacles. First Julio was on the West Coast, almost a continent away from Larry and myself in the East. Another problem was that the series, extended through several months, might be hard for the reader to follow in continuity.

In time, Julio Kaplan left chess teaching to do chess computer programming. Larry D. Evans stopped producing his columns two years later to deal in fine arts. I remained and have written all the ABCs since the latter part of 1982.

Growing understanding of our readership necessarily resulted in metamorphosis of the column, catalyzed by the changing editorial stance. Burt Hochberg's departure in 1979 brought in successive chiefs: Fairfield Hoban, Frank Elley, and Larry Parr. These creative and talented men lent the ABCs their unique perspectives and overviews while retaining its initial intentions.

Ever since 1977, when I wrote my first ABCs, I have concentrated on problems that students actually encounter as they play, rather than on purely theoretical matters. As a teacher, I've learned to take nothing for granted. I assume a student's ignorance, so as to avoid gaps in his learning. Examples have been selected and arranged with meticulous care. Sometimes this meant winnowing as few as seven positions from over two hundred initial selections for an article. Often several weeks of research preceded the writing of a single sentence. Great emphasis has been placed on the *reasons* for the moves, and most concepts are spelled out in both words and variations.

Since the column copes with practical problems, I've devised original remedial techniques and drawn upon my extensive experience in correcting student errors and handicaps. Many suggestions are contained in the columns for students who wish to continue their study independently of the article in question, and teachers may find this material helpful in structuring their own courses.

Anyway, here are my fifty best columns from the ABCs series. They cover every aspect of chess from the opening to middlegame to endgame, from strategy to tactics. Use them to improve your understanding and play. You could browse around to whatever subject interests you, but it's more instructive to read from start to finish. The complete course of study here given was developed over time in my classes and private lessons. In the lexicon of chess, these are the fundamentals, or, if you will, the ABCs.

1

FUNDAMENTALS

THE 64 COMMANDMENTS

A Summary of Hints, Pointers and Precepts from the ABCs

The following sixty-four practical suggestions have been extracted from many different ABC columns. Traditional distinctions between open and closed games have been disregarded, and the principles now appear in terms of difficulty from basic to advanced.

A word of caution. Chess teachers phrase principles in positive, straightforward terms to make them easier to remember. But they are really nothing more than general guidelines for good play. They often suggest the right move, but you must always make your own decisions based on the given circumstances as well.

Should you ever break a principle? The answer is *yes*, but only if you have a specific reason for doing so. Without such a concrete reason, the answer is probably *no*.

1. Be aggressive, but play soundly. Don't take unnecessary chances.

2. Make sure every move has a purpose.
3. If you know you opponent's style, take advantage of it. But, in the final analysis, play the board, not the player.
4. Don't ignore your opponent's moves.
5. Don't give needless checks. Check only when it makes sense.
6. Answer all threats. Try to do so by improving your position and/or posing a counterthreat.
7. Play for the initiative. If you already have it, maintain it. If you don't have it, seize it.
8. When exchanging, try to get at least as much as you give up.
9. Take with the man of least value, unless there is a definite reason for doing otherwise.
10. Cut your losses. If you must lose material, lose as little as possible.
11. If you blunder, don't give up fighting. After getting the advantage, your opponent may relax and let you escape.
12. Never play a risky move, hoping your opponent will overlook your threat, unless you have a losing position. In that case, you have nothing to lose.
13. Rely on your own powers. If you can't see the point of your opponent's move, assume there isn't any.
14. Don't sacrifice without good reason.
15. When you can't determine whether to accept or decline a sacrifice, accept it.
16. Attack in number. Don't rely on just one or two pieces.
17. Look for double attacks.
18. Play for the center: guard it, occupy it, influence it.
19. Fight for the center with pawns.
20. Don't make careless pawn moves. In the opening, move as few pawns as necessary to complete your development.
21. If feasible, move both center pawns two squares each.
22. In the opening, move only center pawns, unless the opening system or situation requires otherwise.
23. Try to develop your Bishops before blocking them in by moving a center pawn just one square.
24. Develop your pieces quickly, preferably toward the center (especially Knights, which often are "grim on the rim").
25. Develop purposefully, and not just for development's sake.
26. Don't waste time or moves. Try to develop a new piece on each turn. Don't move a piece twice in the opening without good reason.

27. Try to develop with threats, but don't threaten pointlessly.
28. Develop minor pieces early. Kingside pieces should usually be developed sooner than Queenside ones, and Knights before Bishops.
29. Develop during exchanges.
30. To exploit an advantage in development, attack.
31. In the opening, don't remove your Queen from play to "win" a pawn.
32. Don't bring out the Queen too early, unless the natural course of play requires it.
33. Try to give as much scope to your pieces as possible.
34. Seize open lines.
35. Develop Rooks to open files, or to files likely to open.
36. Castle early.
37. Try to prevent your opponent's King from castling. Keep it trapped in the center, especially In open games.
38. Try to pin your opponent's pieces. Avoid pins against your own pieces.
39. Don't capture pinned pieces until you can benefit from doing so. If possible, try to attack them again, especially with pawns.
40. After castling, don't move the pawns in front of your King without specific reason.
41. To attack the King, pick a target square around it.
42. When applicable, pick target squares on the color of your unopposed Bishop. (Bishops control squares of only one color. If you have a Bishop that controls dark squares and your opponent has exchanged his corresponding Bishop, your dark-squared Bishop is "unopposed" on those squares.)
43. Look for tactics especially on squares of the color controlled by your unopposed Bishop.
44. Try to avoid early exchanges of Bishops for Knights.
45. Double your attacking pieces by building batteries (two or more pieces of like power attacking along the same line). Put Queen and Rook(s) on the same file or rank, and Queen and Bishop on the same diagonal.
46. Build batteries with the less valuable men up front, unless tactics require otherwise.
47. Maximize the efficiency of your moves. Play flexibly.
48. To strengthen control of a file, double your major pieces (Rooks and/or Queen) on it.

49. Determine whether you have an open or closed game, and play accordingly.
50. Usually play to retain your Bishops in open games, and sometimes Knights in closed games.
51. To improve the scope of your Bishop, place your pawns on squares opposite in color to it.
52. Keep your weaknesses on the color opposite to that of your opponent's strongest Bishop.
53. Trade when ahead in material or when under attack, unless you have a sound reason for doing otherwise. Avoid trades when behind in material or when attacking.
54. Choose a plan and stay with it. Change it only if you should or must.
55. To gain space, you usually have to sacrifice time.
56. If cramped, free your game by exchanging material.
57. Trade bad minor pieces for good ones.
58. If the position is unsettled, disguise your plans; make non-committal moves.
59. To gain space or open lines, advance pawns.
60. If the center is blocked, don't automatically castle.
61. If behind in development, keep the game closed.
62. Try to accumulate small advantages.
63. Try to dominate the seventh rank, especially with Rooks.
64. Use the analytic method. When you don't know what to do, first evaluate the position (as best you can), then ask pertinent questions about your analysis.

THICK OF THE ACTION

Experience Has Shown That, All Other Things Being Equal, the Center Is Definitely "Where It's At"

It's a fundamental principle to play for the center. *Center* refers to the four squares in the very middle of the board (d4, d5, e4, and e5) and the 12 squares immediately surrounding them (c3, c4, c5, c6, d6, e6, f6, f5, f4, f3, e3, and d3). There's a significance to this region, but first you should understand what "playing" for the center means.

You can play for the center by:
- Occupying it (placing pieces and pawns on the center squares),
- Controlling it (developing your forces so that they guard the center), or
- Influencing it indirectly by attacking and driving away enemy men that are bearing down on the center.

Much of the time you must rely on all three approaches to dominate the center.

Occupying the center with pieces and pawns has several advantages. Pieces so placed can move to either side of the board more quickly and easily than they usually can when posted near the edge. The center gives them greater flexibility. Furthermore, by occupying the center (and supporting the occupying men with other attackers), you make it harder for your opponent to organize and coordinate his own forces.

Centralized pieces also have greater mobility (more squares to move to). To observe this, compare like pieces occupying a1 and d4 on an otherwise empty board. From d4, a Knight can move to 8 different squares, a Bishop 13, a Rook 14, a Queen 27, and a King 8. From a1, a Knight attacks only 2 squares, a Bishop 7, a Rook 14, a Queen 21, and a King 3. Except for the Rook (which attacks 14 squares no matter where it sits on a clear board), every piece's scope increases as it nears the center.

The value of center occupation is clear in this position from Stolberg–Botvinnik:

Mikhail Botvinnik

White to move

Stolberg

MOSCOW 1940

Black's central predominance gives him mastery over the position. He can literally do anything he wants, attacking anywhere he pleases. It's as if his pieces are using the center and the supporting d-pawn as a resting place. Even though White's pieces are not hemmed in by Black's pawns, they are enormously restricted by Black's power in the middle.

1. Nb2 Rc3 2. Bd2 Rb3 3. Qc2 Qb5 4. Rc1 Bf8 5. Rd1 Re2 6. Qc1 Rxh3 +! 7. gxh3 d4 White resigns.

White is helpless against the threat of 8 ... Qd5 followed by 9 ... Qg2.

White stands equally badly in the following from Ortega–Korchnoi:

Viktor Korchnoi

Black to move

Rogelio Ortega

HAVANA 1963

Once again, Black's pieces are powerfully poised, and this time fronted by menacing pawns that cramp White even further. Korchnoi's central superiority led to a material edge after ...

1... d3!

Clearing the a7-g1 diagonal.

2. cxd3 e3!

Threatening 3... Qxg2 mate.

3. Bf3 exf2 + 4. Kxf2 Ng4 + 5. Kg1

Here 5. Bxg4? loses to 5... Qxg2 + 6. Ke3 Bxf4 +

7. Kxf4 Qf2 + 8. Kg5 (8. Ke5 is met by 8... Qf6 mate) 8... Qf6 + 9. Kh5 g6 + 10. Kh6 g5 + 11. Kh5 Qg6 mate.

5... Qd4 + 6. Be3

Worse is 6. Kh1 Nf2 + 7. Kg1 Nh3 + 8. Kh1 Qg1 + 9. Rxg1 Nf2 mate.

6... Nxe3 7. Qxe3 Qxe3 + 8. Rxe3 Bc5

Here Black must win at least the exchange (a Rook for a minor piece).

Guarding the center can be just as important as attacking it. In fact, central occupation doesn't necessarily mean central control, for a single piece or pawn does not protect itself or the square it occupies. Contrast a Black Bishop at e4 with one at b7. The centralized piece guards more squares (13 to 9), but both Bishops control the same number along the a8-h1 diagonal.

Furthermore, the Bishop on e4 doesn't protect that important central square. A Bishop in the center may even be more subject to attack (though the greater flexibility is usually worth the risk). This somewhat explains the rationale of hyper-modern play: instead of occupying the center immediately, pressure is first concentrated against it, especially by a flanked Bishop.

A pawn may exert the strongest hold over a square, for generally you can't afford exchanging a piece for such a weak unit.

In this position, White's Knight cannot be driven from d5 (if exchanged, it could be replaced by another piece), whereas Black's Knight must retreat when threatened by White's less valuable c-pawn.

If you can't immediately occupy or attack the center, you may be able to influence it indirectly by harassing enemy men that affect it. This is the case with the Nimzo-Indian Defense (1. d4 Nf6 2. c4 e6 3.Nc3 Bb4). White's third move threatens 4. e4, and Black's Bishop at b4 prevents it—not by attacking e4 itself (as 3 ... d5 does), but by pinning the square's protector (and possibly capturing the Knight if the pin is broken). Since the Bishop's real target is e4, not c3, it's clear that a dark-squared Bishop can actually attack a light square!

Another example is Black's fifth move in the Najdorf Sicilian (1. e4 c5 2. Nf3 d6 3. d4 cxd4 4. Nxd4 Nf6 5. Nc3 a6). One thing 5 ... a6 accomplishes is preparation for a future attack against White's e-pawn. Black may eventually be able to play ... b5, allowing him to post his Bishop at b7, where it can hit the pawn at e4. And, if the timing is right, Black can dislodge the Knight at c3 with the pesky advance ... b4. Since 5 ... a6 lays the foundation for this plan, it's fair to say the move indirectly attacks the center:

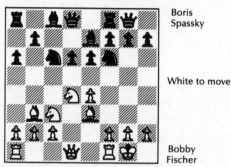

Boris
Spassky

White to move

Bobby
Fischer

FOURTH MATCH GAME 1972

This position, reached after **1. e4 c5 2. Nf3 d6 3. d4 cxd4 4. Nxd4 Nf6 5. Nc3 Nc6 6. Bc4 e6 7. Bb3 Be7 8. Be3 0-0 9. 0-0 a6,** shows the evolution of this type of attack:

10. f4 Nxd4 11. Bxd4 b5

Threatening 12... b4.

12. a3 Bb7 13. Qd3.

Spassky now decided to renew the pressure against the e-pawn.

13... a5!

Black threatens 14 ... b4 (both 14. Nxb5, trading the b-pawn for the e-pawn, and 14. Qxb5 Ba6 are undesirable for White).

Whether it's the opening, middlegame, or endgame (yes, even here, centralize your pieces, especially your King), the middle of the board is the center of action. So play for the center: Occupy it, guard it, and influence it.

CONVENTIONAL WISDOM

It May Be One of the Oldest Bits of Chess Advice, But It's Still an Invaluable Guide for Opening Play

"Knights before Bishops" is an aphorism familiar to chess players everywhere. It means, simply, that in the opening you should develop Knights before Bishops.

Logic supports this. As long-range pieces, Bishops can sweep across the board instantly; they don't have to be up close to attack or defend. The slower-moving Knights must be near the target to work their magic. After 1. e4 e5, for example, compare White's KN, which needs two moves to attack f7 (say, N-f3-g5), to White's KB, which can do the job in one move (Bc4). As you can see, it makes sense to start the shorter-scoped Knights on their way sooner than Bishops.

Knight moves in the opening also tend to be less committal than Bishop moves. Consider White's KN. It has three possible first moves after 1. e4 e5 (to h3, e2, or f3), but in the overwhelming majority of cases, it is played to f3. Space is the primary reason. At f3 a Knight influences eight squares (h2, g1, e1, d2, d4, e5, g5, h4), while at e2 it observes six; at h3 it guards only four. Remember the maxim: *A Knight on the rim is grim.*

Regardless of the opening, you should develop your KN most of the time to f3 (or f6, of course, if you're playing Black). By doing so before moving the KB, you're usually not giving away too much about your game plan. Early development of the KB, however, reveals a lot more. Depending on the opening system, the KB has a number of good posts to choose from. In fact, its placement often determines the opening set-up.

In the Ruy Lopez (1. e4 e5 2. Nf3 Nc6 3. Bb5), moving the KB heralds White's plan of pressuring the center by attacking the Knight that guards d4 and e5. Or, the Bishop could direct the assault on f7, a role it assumes in both the Giuoco Piano (1. e4 e5 2. Nf3 Nc6 3. Bc4 Bc5) and the Two Knights Defense (3 ... Nf6). From d3, the

Bishop bears on the key square e4 and attacks along the b1-h7 diagonal, as in the Petroff Defense (1. e4 e5 2. Nf3 Nf6 3. Nxe5 d6 4. Nf3 Nxe4 5. d4 d5 6. Bd3). In Alekhine's Defense (1. e4 Nf6), White's KB is often developed quietly to e2 (1. e4 Nf6 2. e5 Nd5 3. d4 d6 4. Nf3 Bg4 5. Be2). Here it breaks the pin, setting up the trap 5 ... Bxf3 (removing the Knight so that White must recapture on e5 with a pawn—Black thinks) 6. Bxf3 dxe5? 7. c4! The KB can even be developed on the flank, as in the Najdorf variation of the Sicilian Defense (1. e4 c5 2. Nf3 d6 3. d4 cxd4 4. Nxd4 Nf6 5. Nc3 a6, and now 6. g3). At g2, the Bishop helps discourage Black's usual freeing move, ... d5.

All these examples are KP openings. In each case the KN is developed before the KB. The natural conclusion is that developing the KN first is less committal and in harmony with the principle of Knights before Bishops. And that it is.

Nevertheless, like nearly everything in chess, this principle is far from absolute. Several factors—the choice of opening, the color you are playing, and the dynamics of a particular position—can affect your choice. It's a bad habit to follow such a principle blindly. In applying the principle, novices might play nothing but the Four Knights Defense (1. e4 e5 2. Nf3 Nc6 3. Nc3 Nf6), a lifeless, limited opening that, played too much, can stultify a newcomer's growth.

Eventually, many players adopt a modified principle. Instead of developing both Knights before either Bishop, they follow this formula: first the KN, then the KB, then the QN, then the QB. This approach, probably most applicable after 1. e4, is still too rigid; it doesn't weigh the differences between KP and QP openings.

KP openings generally produce open and semi-open centers, where the King is more exposed. Getting out the Kingside pieces first means the King can be gotten to safety sooner. Because QP openings tend to be more closed, King safety may not be initially as important as other factors. For example, if after 1. d4 d5 White developed his Kingside pieces immediately (2. Nf3 followed by 3. e3), he would block in his QB. In a popular line, White avoids this by developing the QB before moving the e-pawn (1. d4 d5 2. c4 e6 3. Nc3 Nf6 4. Bg5 Nbd7 5. e3). Here we see White has the time to develop his Queenside minor pieces before his Kingside ones.

In QP openings, some players bring out their Queenside minor pieces first, but still follow the principle too mechanically. After 1. d4 d5 some beginners try 2. Nc3 instead of the usual 2. c4, a useful move that gains Queenside space and attacks the center. This

Knight move is premature. It blocks the c-pawn and leads to a cramped game. One can completely misplay an opening by rigidly following any formula. (Granted, there is a currently popular line with 1. d4 d5 2. Nc3, but only seasoned players are advised to try this double-edged plan.)

Black will find the Knights-before-Bishops principle somewhat less helpful than White. For example, in one line of the Caro-Kann Defense (1. e4 c6 2. d4 d5 3. Nc3 dxe4 4. Nxe4 Bf5), Black develops his QB before any of his other minor pieces. This is done to avoid blocking the Bishop; the vital ... e6 must be played soon, so Black frees his QB at the first opportunity. Otherwise, the QB will be "trapped" behind a wall of its own pawns. In the Winawer French Defense (1.e4 e6 2. d4 d5 3. Nc3 Bb4), Black develops his KB right away to pin the Knight and attack the White center (notice that the pinned Knight is no longer guarding d5 and e4).

Like all principles, this one has its exceptions. It can't tell you the next move, but in some situations it might help you look in the right direction. So, the next time you're stuck, remember: Knights before Bishops.

FEMININE MYSTIQUE

Many Players Suffer from a Common Delusion: That They Know How to Treat the Lady

Give some people a chess problem and the first thing they do is reach for the Queen, often without thinking. Inexperienced players in particular rely on the Queen so much they'll do almost anything not to trade it. A common delusion is to believe one can handle the Queen better than the other forces. This makes little sense, for the Queen actually is a Rook and Bishop combined. Surely one should first understand its component forces before being able to appreciate the Queen itself.

The greatest misuse of the Queen occurs in the opening, when both sides are grappling for an advantage, fighting for the center, developing pieces, and safeguarding the King. Because of the Queen's ability to strike suddenly with multiple attacks, it's tempting to bring it out immediately. But the Queen is just one piece. The Queen's force radiates in all directions, but it can attack a specific square only once. To be effective, the Queen must work in a battery with support troops.

Timing is important. Because you can usually bring out the Queen at a moment's notice, it's undesirable to tip your hand by developing it right away. Bishops and Knights, however, have fewer good squares at their disposal. They take longer to reach their ideal spots, especially Knights. Moreover, minor pieces are less valuable than the Queen and therefore harder to harass. They can be placed in outpost positions without as much fear of being driven away.

When brought out too early, the Queen is easily vulnerable to attack. Because of the Queen's relative value, you will probably have to move it every time it's challenged (unless the assailant is the opposing Queen). Your opponent thereby builds his game at your expense, menacing the prematurely developed Queen while at the same time bringing out his own forces.

Consider the Center Counter Defense (1. e4 d5). After 2. exd5 Qxd5, White gains a tempo with 3. Nc3. To stress the absurdity of trying to keep the Queen centralized, many teachers show students the following line: 3 ... Qd4? 4. Nf3 (developing with a gain of time) 4 ... Qc5? 5. d4 (opening more lines for development at Black's expense) 5 ... Qc6?? 6. Bb5, winning the hapless Queen

But Diagram 1 gives a better and more realistic example:

MOBILE 1855
Giuoco Piano

A.B. Meek   Paul Morphy

---

1. e4 e5 2. Nf3 Nc6 3. Bc4 Bc5 4. d4
exd4 5.Ng5 Nh6 6.Nxf7 Nxf7 7.Bxf7 Kxf7 8.Qh5 g6 9.Qxc5

White has regained his sacrificed material and forced the Black King to move. But the Black King is not really endangered now,

DIAGRAM 1

while the White Queen, having been prematurely developed, is susceptible to pesky attacks:

9 ... d6 10. Qb5 Re8

Preparing if necessary, to castle by hand.

11. Qb3 +

A meaningless, time-wasting check.

11 ... d5 12. f3 Na5 13. Qd3 dxe4 14. fxe4 Qh4 +

Having first developed his other forces, Black now thrusts his Queen into the fray, with decisive effect.

15. g3 Rxe4 +

This is better than swapping Queens by 15 ... Qxe4+ 16. Qxe4 Rxe4+, though that also wins.

16. Kf2 Qe7 17. Nd2 Re3 18. Qb5

Of course, 18. Qxd4 would allow 18 ... Re2 +, a devastating seventh-rank invasion (19. Kg1 Re1 + 20.Kg2 Qe2 + 21.Qf2, and now Black can choose either 21 ... Qxf2 + and 22 ... Rxh1 or 21 ... Bh3 + and 22 ... Qxf2.

18 ... c6 19. Qf1

Again, 19. Qxa5 permits 19 ... Re2 +.

19 ... Bh3!

You guessed it; 20. Qxh3 is answered by 20 ... Re2 +.

20. Qd1

Think of it: White's Queen has made eight moves to reach its original square! What an incredible waste of time.

20 ... Rf8 21. Nf3 Ke8, White resigns.

White resigned in view of 22. Bxe3 Qxe3, mate—a beautiful exploitation of premature Queen development.

Early development of the Queen is usually bad, but not always. Sometimes bringing out the Queen in the first few moves happens naturally and is the right idea, especially if the other side can't exploit it.

Compare the following two situations: (Diagram A) 1. e4 e5 2.d4 exd4 3. Qxd4

DIAGRAM A

(Diagram B) 1. e4 e5 2. Nf3 Nc6 3.d4 exd4 4. Nxd4 Nxd4? 5. Qxd4

DIAGRAM B

In *A*, White's Queen is prematurely developed, and Black can attack it by 3 ... Nc6, which develops the Knight with a gain of time. By having to move his Queen again, White loses his first-move advantage.

In *B*, White's Queen is out because it had to recapture on d4. Even though the Queen occupies a central square, Black has no useful way to dislodge it; having already exchanged his Queen-Knight. Black can drive away the Queen with 5 ... c5, but this doesn't really contribute to his development. It also has the drawback of weakening the squares d5 and d6, which could never again be guarded by a pawn. White might then be able to occupy d5 (say, with a Knight) and exert enormous pressure along the d-file (picture a Black pawn at d6 and White Rooks at d1 and d2). Thus, here Black has no satisfactory way to attack d4, and White's Queen can remain perched in the center.

In the opening, mobilize your forces as soon as possible, especially your Bishops and Knights. Attack with several pieces, not just with the Queen, which really needs support to get the job done. And try not to bring out the Queen too early. That approach seldom works (except for when it does).

AGGRESSIVE SAFETY

Sure, Castling Is a Defensive Move. But Sometimes You Can Make It Do Double Duty

Because the King is the most vulnerable piece, and because castling always involves shifting the King from the center (which is generally exposed) to one of the wings (which are generally sheltered), it is natural to think of castling as a defensive maneuver. But clearly it is a developing move as well, for it connects the Rooks, preparing them for play in the center. Therefore, castling can also be an offensive weapon. Here are several of the more common themes:

• *Castling for direct attack.* Sometimes a player castles expressly to give a direct attack with the Rook, as in this game, played at Rook odds:

NEW ORLEANS 1858
Two Knights' Defense

Paul Morphy   Amateur

Remove White's Queen-Rook.
1.e4 e5 2. Nf3 Nc6 3. Bc4 Nf6 4. Ng5 d5 5. exd5 Nxd5 6. Nxf7 Kxf7

7.Qf3+ Ke6 8. Nc3 Nd4 9. Bxd5+ Kd6 10. Qf7 Be6 11. Bxe6 Nxe6 12.
Ne4+ Kd5 13.c4+ Kxe4 14. Qxe6 Qd4 15. Qg4+ Kd3 16. Qe2+ Kc2
17.d3+ Kxc1.
White can now mate on the move by playing the "defensive" ...
18. 0-0 mate.

• *Castling to exploit the f-file.* One often castles Kingside to place
a Rook on an open or half-open f-file (an open file is free of all
pawns; a half-open file is free of your own pawns but has at least
one enemy pawn). Some openings, such as the King's Gambit (1. e4
e5 2. f4), are designed to take advantage of the half-open f-file, with
the focal point usually being the squares f2 or f7. This game shows a
thematic, but unexpected, way to utilize the f-file:

WARSAW 1844
Giuoco Piano

Hoffman   Petroff

1. e4 e5 2. Nf3 Nc6 3. Bc4 Bc5 4.c3 Nf6 5. d4 exd4 6. e5 Ne4 7. Bd5
Nxf2 8. Kxf2 dxc3+ 9. Kg3 cxb2 10. Bxb2 Ne7 11. Ng5 Nxd5 12. Nxf7
Facing what seems to be a devastating fork, Black found the
amazing ...
12 ... O-O!!
... leaving his Queen hanging and attacking along the f-file. Now
on 13. Qxd5 Rxf7, White has no defense against either 14 ... Bf2+
(supporting a Queen invasion at h4) or 14 ... Qg5+ (forcing the King
into a discovered check along the c8-h3 diagonal).
**13. Nxd8 Bf2+ 14. Kh3 d6+ 15. e6 Nf4+ 16. Kg4 Nxe6 17. g3
Nxd8+ 18. Kg5 Rf5+ 19. Kg4 Rf6+ 20. Kh4 Rf4+ 21. Kg5 Ne6+ 22.
Kh5 g6+ 23. Kh6 Rh4+ 24. gxh4 Be3 mate.**

• *Castling to attack along the e-file.* This is perhaps the most
common idea, particularly when the e-file is open and the other
side's King is unable to leave the center quickly enough. Sometimes
the opposing King is not immediately endangered because it is
shielded by one or more of its own men. In such cases, the castler's
real threat is to pin these men to their King by playing Re1 for White
or Re8 for Black:

NEW YORK 1857
King's Gambit

Schulten   Morphy

1. e4 e5 2. f4 d5 3.exd5 e4 4.Nc3 Nf6 5.d3 Bb4 6. Bd2 e3 7.Bxe3

Morphy has sacrificed his center pawns to speed up development and open attacking routes to White's King, which cannot leave the center for at least a couple of moves. After ...

7 ... 0-0

... White, concerned with the possible pin of his Bishop along the e-file, retreated.

8. Bd2

Using his open lines, especially the e-file, Morphy concluded incisively:

8 ... Bxc3

This removes a key defender of the square e2.

9. bxc3

Keeping the Bishop at d2 so that e3 is not weakened.

9 ... Re8+ 10. Be2 Bg4 11. c4 c6 12. dxc6 Nxc6

Threatening to exploit the pin on the e-file by 13 ... Nd4.

13. Kf1 Rxe2! 14. Nxe2 Nd4

White gets out of one pin and into another.

15. Qb1 Bxe2+ 16. Kf2 Ng4+ 17. Kg1

After 17. Kg3 Nf5 + 18. Kh3, both 18 ... Nf2 and 18 ... Qh4 are mate.

17 ... Nf3+ 18. gxf3 Qd4+ 19. Kg2 Qf2+ 20. Kh3 Qxf3+ 21. Kh4 Nh6

Threatening 22 ... Qg4 mate.

22. Qg1 Nf5+ 23.Kg5 Qh5 mate.

The key to this attack was Black's ability to castle quickly and control the e-file with his Rook. Sometimes you can combine attack and defense along the e-file by castling Kingside (diagram).

Black had played 1 ... Qg4 on the previous move, forking the pawns at e4 and g2. White can turn the situation to his advantage with the aggressive 2.0-0. The point is that 2. Qxe4 allows White to

pin the Queen by 3. Rel. This type of indirect defense and counterattack, where the castler saves himself by threatening a pin along
the e-file, occurs in a lot of different openings. Many instances, in
particular, can be found in variations of the Ruy Lopez (1. e4
e5 2. Nf3 Nc6 3.Bb5).
• *Castling Queenside to seize the d-file.* When it is feasible and
you are prepared to castle in either direction, occupying the d-file at
once by castling Queenside can save a tempo. After that, it takes
only one more move to place Rooks on both central files, while you
require two more moves to do the same after Kingside castling. In
this game, White castled Queenside for the sake of immediate
tactics along the d-file:

PARIS 1858
Philidor's Defense

Morphy   *Duke of Brunswick*

**1.e4 e5 2. Nf3 d6 3. d4 Bg4 4. dxe5 Bxf3 5. Qxf3 dxe5 6. Bc4 Nf6 7.
Qb3 Qe7 8. Nc3 c6 9. Bg5 b5 10. Nxb5 cxb5 11. Bxb5+ Nbd7**
Morphy maintained his initiative here with ... **12.0-0-0**
Which got his King out of the way and also threatened the Knight
at d7. This immediate seizure of the d-file soon proved decisive after
...
12 ... Rd8 13. Rxd7! Rxd7 14. Rd1
Continuing to use the d-file.
14. ... Qe6 15. Bxd7+ Nxd7 16. Qb8+!! Nxb8 17.Rd8 mate.
As explained earlier, Queenside castling occasionally enables the
attacker to influence both central files. A memorable example:

VIENNA 1910
Caro-Kann Defense

Richard Reti   *Saviely Tartakower*

**1. e4 c6 2. d4 d5 3. Nc3 dxe4 4. Nxe4 Nf6
5. Qd3 e5 6. dxe5 Qa5+ 7.Bd2 Qxe5**
Black is pinning and twice attacking White's Knight at e4. Unwit-
tingly, he has forced White to go ahead with his plan to castle
Queenside. The game went on, but not for long.
8.0-0-0!

Preventing 8 ... Qxe4 because of the pin 9. Re1—thank you, e-file.
8 ... Nxe4 9.Qd8 +!! Kxd8 10.Bg5 +
This double check, based on the discovery along the d-file set up
by castling Queenside, is immediately decisive.
10. ... Kc7
If 10... Ke8, then 11. Rd8 is still mate—thank you, d-file.
11. Bd8 mate.

NO FREE LUNCH

If You Go Looking for Handouts, Don't Expect to Win Many Games

Despite a popular misconception, strong chessplayers seldom win
in less than ten moves. Even when playing against a novice, a master
will ordinarily take fifteen to twenty moves to force mate. Ironically,
an average player may beat a like opponent in fewer moves, but also
will lose games in the process by taking foolhardy chances that
backfire. For a game to end in less than ten moves, at least one of
the two combatants must err badly. Consider the shortest game
possible, the "Fool's Mate:"
1. f3? e5 2. g4?? Qh4 mate.
Anyone from rank beginner to world champion could win this
game, but only an unschooled player could lose it. Of the 19 moves
available to White on his second turn, only one permits immediate
mate (2. h3 allows mate in two). Ability clearly is not necessarily
reflected in how quickly you win.
Sometimes the quick winner does have some knowhow and tries
to set an unsound trap. This tactic works only if the defender misses
what is usually an obvious threat. The "Scholar's Mate," a favorite of
youngsters everywhere, is an example:
1.e4 e5 2. Bc4 Nc6 3. Qf3? Nd4?? 4. Qxf7 mate.

It succeeds only if Black overlooks or ignores the attack on his f-pawn. If Black plays 3 ... Nf6, however, he gets the advantage, for White's Queen is out of place and subject to harassment. The Queen on f3 also deprives the KN of its best square. To win in this quick way, White has to play a bad move, hoping for a blunder. And that's foolhardy.

A strong player would never play so unsoundly, violating the spirit of the opening in a vainglorious attempt to win quickly. He is content simply to build his game, accumulating advantage after advantage until his attack is irresistible—until he can *force* a win.

Newcomers may not easily grasp the concept of forced responses. You force your opponent's reply if, in answer to your move, he has: (1) only one legal move; (2) a couple of legal moves, all of which, along with their consequences, you can see in your head; or (3) an indefinite number of moves, of which only a few are feasible because they alone allow the opponent to avoid immediate harm.

If you could not force your opponent's moves, you could not look ahead. You could not calculate combinations, employ tactics, or play out any attacking sequence. Strong players are not interested in risky, haphazard opening checkmates, but in tactical variations that win by force. To arrive at these, you must first develop your position, and this usually takes more than ten moves.

Young players particularly are prone to move without thinking about forcing their opponent's response. Natural impulsiveness may be to blame, but early training also plays a role. Even popular textbooks encourage reckless play by offering examples without regard to natural logic. One respected work introduces the "smothered mate" this way (without the question marks or comments):

1.c4 Nc6 2. e3? Ne5?

Threatening and forcing nothing.

3. Ne2??

The only move allowing mate in one.

3 ... Nd3 mate.

Since no admonitions are given against playing Black's second move, the writer is at least implying (and, to the inexperienced, advocating) this type of risky approach to chess. A far better example is a game of Alexander Alekhine's that took only six moves:

1. e4 c6 2. d4 d5 3. Nc3 dxe4 4. Nxe4 Nd7 5. Qe2 Ngf6 6. Nd6 mate.

While White's fifth move may not objectively be the best, it does fit the plan of castling Queenside and at least makes some sense. Even Black's error was based on his preoccupation with avoiding doubled f-pawns (which is why he played 4 ... Nd7). White did not play 5. Qe2 solely with the hope of giving a smothered mate (as Black does in the previous example by 2 ... Ne5?). It was merely an extra pitfall—part of a greater plan—that Black failed to sidestep.

Students: Never play moves that you know to be bad in the hope your opponent will err and allow you to win quickly. First develop your game using the principles of good opening play. Get the advantage, and then you can win—by force.

Teachers: Never give a bad example to illustrate a concept. Give the best example you know. You can always vary your explanation to meet the individual needs of the student. Even if your students don't quite understand the example, you will still be encouraging good habits and therefore helping to develop their play.

THE ENDGAME

What Is an Ending? When Does It Begin?

Since the flow of a game never stops, the ending is not independent of the opening or the middlegame but is the logical outcome of both. Some openings (such as the Exchange Lopez) are played with a specific view toward a favorable ending. Moreover, the phases (opening, middlegame, endgame) are not separated by clear boundaries. They are connected by transitions which are difficult to define precisely. The game should be thought of as an organic whole, for each phase is closely linked to the others. The ending is the part in which one can finally exploit the advantages accumulated in the opening and middlegame.

Although all this is very true, it is still useful to make some general statements about endings. They differ from openings and middlegames in the following ways (these are not hard and fast rules):

1. Less material is on the board (the Queen is usually gone).
2. They lend themselves to exact calculation.
3. The relative values of the pieces are changed (this is especially true of pawns and minor pieces).
4. Material advantages are emphasized.
5. It is often desirable not to move.
6. The active participation of the King is required.

Of these six statements, it is the last with which we are most concerned here. Because the material on the board is reduced and a surprise mating attack is unlikely, the King is able to play a more active role than in the opening and the middlegame. It should be developed toward the center or to some other important area. If both White and Black have the same objective, however, clearly at least one cannot succeed. As the Kings approach each other, how can we determine which will be more powerful?

The answer lies in the relationship between the two Kings, which is known as the *opposition*. Consider the following position: W: Ke4 B: Ke6 (this means that the White King is on e4 and the Black King is on e6). If it is White's turn to play, which King stands better? A quick examination shows that Black does, because if White plays Kf4, Black can choose between Kf6, holding off the White King, or Kd5, advancing. Also, if White plays Kd4, Black can choose between the defensive Kd6 or the attacking Kf5. White goes first, but Black decides what is to follow. In this case, it is said that Black has the opposition. Put simply, the Kings stand in opposition if

1. they occupy squares of the same color, AND
2. They are separated by an odd number of squares (1, 3, or 5) along a rank, file, or diagonal.

You have the opposition if the above two conditions are fulfilled and if it is your opponent's turn to move. If the Kings do not stand in opposition, whoever moves can take either the direct, distant, diagonal, or rectangular opposition.

Examples of Various Kinds of Opposition

Direct opposition:	1. W:Kd4	B:Kd6
	2. W:Kd4	B:Kf4
Distant opposition:	3. W:Ke2	B:Ke6
	4. W:Ke2	B:Ke8

	5. W:Kg2	B:Kc2
	6. W:Kg2	B:Ka2
Diagonal opposition:	7. W:Kh1	B:Kf3
	8. W:Kh1	B:Kd5
	9. W:Kh1	B:Kb7

Rectangular opposition is a special case, and must be considered separately. If the Kings are not on the same straight line, but are on squares of the same color, then draw the smallest possible rectangle containing the two Kings: if both the long and short sides of the rectangle are odd in number, then the Kings stand in rectangular opposition and whoever doesn't move has the advantage.

Rectangular opposition:	10. W:Ke2	B:Kc6
	11. W:Ka8	B:Kc2
	12. W:Kc1	B:Kg7

Now let's look at concrete examples.

13. W:Kf6, Pe6; B:Kf8.

In King and pawn vs. King endings it is crucial to have the opposition when the pawn reaches the 6th rank. In this case, neither player wants to move—an example of mutual zugzwang. Zugzwang is a situation in which having the move is a decided disadvantage. If White moves he only draws because Black has the opposition: 1. e7+ Ke8 2. Ke6 is stalemate. If Black moves he loses because White has the opposition: 1 ... Ke8 2. e7 Kd7 3. Kf7 and wins.

14. W:Ke3, Pe2; B:Ke5.

This is another example of mutual zugzwang. If White has the move it's only a draw: 1. Kf3 (or Kd3) Kf5 (maintaining the opposition) 2. e3 (temporarily seizing the opposition, but his own pawn will prevent him from keeping it) 2 ... Ke5 3. e4 Ke6 (Black draws by staying in front of the pawn on the same file and by opposing the White King every time it advances) 4.Kf4 Kf6 5.e5 + Ke7 (or ... Ke6). 6. Kf5 Kf7 7 . e6 + Ke8 (or ... Ke7) 8. Kf6 Kf8 arriving at # 13. If Black moves first he loses: 1 ... Kd5 (or ... Kf5) 2. Kf4 Ke6 3. Ke4 Kd6 (or ... Kf6) 4.Kf5 Ke7 (or 4 ... Kd5 5. e4 + Kd6 6.Kf6 transposes into the main line) 5. Ke5 Kd7 6. Kf6 Kd6 7 . e4 Kd7 8. e5 Ke8 9. Ke6 Kf8 (or ... Kd8) 10.Kd7 and wins.

The next examples carry it along:

15. W: Ka3, Pg2; B: Kb5. (from the Russian composer Grigoriev)
White to play wins by taking the opposition and maintaining it until reaching a situation similar to #14: 1. Kb3 Kc5 2. Kc3 Kd5 3. Kd3 Ke5 4. Ke3 Kf5 5. Kf3 Kg5 6. Kg3 Kh5 (or ... Kf5) 7 . Kf4 and wins. From this it is clear that the opposition is a tool used in the fight for certain squares.

16. W: Kh4, Pe6; B: Kg7.
White uses the opposition to force a basic win: 1. Kg5 Kg8 (if 1 ... Kf8 2. Kf6 wins) 2. Kg6! (not 2. Kf6? because 2 ... Kf8 then draws) Kf8 3. Kf6 and wins as in #13.

17. W: Ke1, Ph4 & b4; B: Ke8, Ph5 & b5 (by Capablanca).
Whoever moves wins by taking the distant opposition: 1. Ke2! (the Kings are on squares of the same color and are separated by five squares along the Kingfile) 1 ... Ke7 2. Ke3! Ke6 3. Ke4! Kf6 (on 3 ... Kd6 White wins with 4.Kd4) 4.Kf4! (4.Kd5 only draws because Black promotes to a Queen on the same move as White) Kg6 5. Ke5 Kg7 6. Kf5 Kh6 7. Kf6 Kh7 8. Kg5 Kg7 9. Kxh5 Kh7 10. Kg5 Kg7 11. Kf5 and wins by gobbling the QNP.

The opposition is also a key defensive weapon:

18. W: Kg4, Pe4; B: Kh8.
Black to play can draw by taking the distant opposition: 1 ... Kg8! (not 1 ... Kg7? 2. Kg5!) 2. Kf5 Kf7 3. e5 Ke7 drawing as in #14; or 2. Kf4 Kf8 waiting for White to advance also holds the fort.

19. W: Kg2, Pf3; B: Kd1, Pg5 & e5 (by Neustadl).
Here one must be careful to choose the correct opposition. White to play draws by 1. Kh1 (taking the distant opposition). One reasonable continuation is 1 ... Ke2 2. Kg2 Ke3 3. Kg3 Kd3 (trying to trick White into losing the opposition) 4. Kh3 Kd2 (trading pawns draws at once) 5. Kh2 Ke1 6. Kg1 and no progress has been made. If White starts by taking the direct opposition he loses: 1. Kf1? Kd2 2. Kf2 Kd3! (White's own pawn now gets in the way and prevents him from maintaining the opposition) 3. Kg3 Ke3 4. Kg2 Ke2 5. Kg3 Kf1 6. Kg4 Kg2 and wins.

20. W: Ke2, Pf4 & d4; B: Kd5.
Black to play can draw, but not by 1 ... Kxd4? because 2. Kf3 Kd5 3. Kg4 Ke6 4. Kg5 Kf7 5. Kf5 takes the direct opposition and wins, but by taking the direct opposition himself: 1 ... Ke4! 2. Kf2 (on 2. Kd2 Black takes the QP instead) Kxf4!; and if White sacrifices his pawn

right away by 2. d5, Black still draws with 2 ... Kxd5 3. Kf3 Ke6 4. Kg4 Kf6.

The same idea also occurs in this example from Bondarevsky:
21. W: Kf5, Pe6; B: Kg7, Pf6 & d6.
White plays and draws with 1. e7! Kf7 2. e8(Q)+ Kxe8 3. Ke6!

Or how about one from the Korchnoi-Petrosian match in 1974:
22. W: Kg6, Pa4, b3, c4; B: Kg4, Pa5, b6, c5.
White, Korchnoi, won with 1. Kf6 Kf4 2. Ke6 Ke4 3. Kd6 Kd3 4. Kc6 Kc3 5. Kxb6 Kxb3 6. Kb5! and Black doesn't get any of the remaining White pawns!

For the more advanced students, I leave you with an example composed by Botvinnik which Illustrates an oppositional dance of death between the two Kings:
23. W: Kg5, Pd4 & a4; B: Kb7, Pd5, a5, a6.
White wins not by capturing the QP (1. Kf5 Kb6 2. Ke5 Kc6 3. Ke6 Kc7! 4. Kxd5 Kd7 5. Kc5 Kc7 and the pawn on a6 guards a key square and saves Black) but only after winning the RPs by first occupying a8! 1. Kf5! (taking the rectangular opposition) Kb6 2. Kf6! (the distant opposition) Kb7 3. Kf7 Kb8 4. Ke6 Kc7 5. Ke7 (White must resist temptation and not take the QP) Kc6 6. Kd8 Kd6 7. Kc8 Kc6 8. Kb8 Kb6 9. Ka8! and Black will lose everything because his own pawn prevents him from maintaining the direct opposition. Without the extra Black RP White could not win with this maneuver, but would then win by taking the QP as soon as possible.

Whatever else can be said about endings, the opposition concept is basic to most and is therefore a good foundation on which to build endgame knowledge.

2

THE OPENING

FOR OPENERS

An Introduction to the Differences Between King-pawn and Queen-pawn Endings

Most newcomers soon learn that King-pawn and Queen-pawn openings can be very different. A basic contrast is that KP openings generally lead to open and semi-open positions, while QP openings usually are more closed, thus providing fewer opportunities for attack. Since it's easier to become confused by the subtleties of closed games, teachers tend to shy away from introducing QP openings in early lessons.

Why do KP openings generally produce open positions and QP openings closed ones? The answer has a lot to do with the ability to advance both center pawns two squares each. Once this "central break" is accomplished, it's more likely that pawns will be exchanged, leading to a clearing of central lines and an opening of the game. Even if no exchanges take place, the advanced center pawns ensure that White's pieces will have relatively unobstructed ranks, files and diagonals for development. In most games, both players' beginning strategy hinges on their attempts to open up the center in their favor.

After 1. e4, White will soon be able to follow with d4, even if Black tries to stop or discourage it, for the d-pawn starts the game with a natural backup—the Queen. Thus, after 1. e4 e5, White can play (though I'm not recommending it) the immediate 2. d4, because 2. ... exd4 can be answered by 3. Qxd4.

The situation is quite different when White begins with 1. d4. If Black then attacks the e4 square by either 1 ... d5 or 1 ... Nf6, the immediate 2. e4 loses a pawn. The KP simply doesn't have the QP's natural support. In order to open a QP game, White normally has to prepare the e-pawn advance very carefully. This takes time, which largely explains why QP openings seem so slow.

When Black's first move doesn't challenge the e4 square, White can usually advance his KP right away. Thus, after 1. d4 g6, White should play 2. e4. An exception would be if Black answered 1. d4 with 1 ... c5, threatening to trade away White's center pawn. In that case, White might want to keep his QP by first playing 2. d5, deferring the KP advance until the center is secure. (Black could also anticipate 2. e4 by 1 ... f5—the Dutch Defense—but this can be quite risky, especially in view of the Staunton Gambit (2. e4), in which White sacrifices a pawn in return for better development and an attack.

The two most common replies to 1. d4 are 1 ... d5 and 1 ... Nf6. The latter is seen more often nowadays—not because it's inherently better, but because it's more flexible. After 1 ... Nf6, Black has revealed very little about his intentions. He would probably develop his KN to f6 anyway, and meanwhile he hasn't given away his plans about pawn structure and development. For example, is he going to fianchetto his KB or develop it by moving the KP? Will he bring out his QB through the center or fianchetto it to guard e4 from b7?

It's also possible he may still be able to play ... d5, transposing into a double QP game. But Black makes a definite statement if he plays 1 ... d5 instead of 1 ... Nf6. At the very least, 1 ... d5 eliminates the lines where the d-pawn goes to d6. Remember that pawn moves are generally more committal than piece moves: they can't be taken back.

A lot can be learned about QP openings by examining the Queen's Gambit (1. d4 d5 2. c4). Although 2. c4 doesn't really sacrifice a pawn—for reasons we shall soon see—it may not be immediately clear why White plays the move at all. Actually, there are a number of facets to it:

• White gets much more space on the Queenside. Not only will his Queen have access to that wing (at c2, b3 or a4), but the QR should be able to enjoy an open or semi-open c-file.

• White is able to exert more pressure on Black's d-pawn. The full impact of this can be seen by comparing Diagrams 1 and 2. In Diagram 1, Black's d-pawn is quite safe, while in Diagram 2, White has mounted real pressure against it.

• White facilitates the advance of the KP to e4. How? By trying to lure Black's d-pawn out of the center. To this end, White will intensify pressure against d5, hoping to force Black into an unfavorable exchange at c4, surrendering the center. (Though if Black does play 2 ... dxc4, White should first play 3. Nf3, since 3. e4 allows the countersacrifice 3 ... e5.)

DIAGRAM 1

DIAGRAM 2

After 2. c4, Black has several reasonable tries. He could strengthen his center pawn by either 2 ... e6 (the Queen's Gambit Declined) or 2 ... c6 (the Slav Defense). Another possibility is the Queen's Gambit Accepted (2 ... dxc4). Why doesn't 2 ... dxc4 win a pawn? Because Black must compromise his position to hold it.

For example, after 2 ... dxc4 3. e3 (though White has time to play 3. Nf3, stopping 3 ... e5) 3 ... b5 (trying to keep his extra c-pawn) 4. a4 c6 (4 ... a6 fails to 5. axb5, exploiting the pinned a-pawn) 5. axb5 cxb5 6. Qf3, Black must lose a piece.

If 2 ... dxc4 doesn't win a pawn, why does Black play it? The answer is that he intends to follow 2 ... dxc4 soon after with the advance ... c5. This he hopes will lead to either a timely liquidation of the center or the creation of an isolated White d-pawn.

But isolated d-pawns can be two-headed monsters. They have their good and bad points, and so do QP openings.

FOUR KNIGHTS GAME

You Should Probably Avoid This Opening Altogether. But if You Do Play It, You Might as Well Know How

A popular opening for new players is the sequence 1. e4 e5 2. Nf3 Nc6 3. Nc3 Nf6 4. Bc4 Bc5. Sometimes they reverse the order of the third and fourth moves (Diagram 1):

DIAGRAM 1

These moves are played so often partly because of a misapplication of practical chess wisdom. Beginners are urged to play 1. e4 because KP openings are generally the least intricate and most direct of all openings. The drawback is that one may falsely conclude that other first moves (such as 1. d4 or 1. c4) are inferior.

Once the opening has become a double-KP affair (1. e4 e5), the above variation naturally occurs from a superficial interpretation of chess principles. Teachers, after all, recommend rapid development, especially of the minor pieces (and don't forget "Knights before Bishops"). Then they suggest castling to connect the Rooks. These suggestions have great practical value, but if followed blindly they inevitably produce a lifeless variation of the Four Knights Game or Giuoco Pianissimo.

Misuse of the same principles may also persuade one to avoid sharper lines, such as the Giuoco Piano (1. e4 e5 2. Nf3 Nc6 3. Bc4 Bc5 4. c3, which beginners avoid because the QN's best square is temporarily blocked) or the Two Knights Defense (1. e4 e5 2. Nf3 Nc6 3. Bc4 Nf6 4. Ng5, which beginners distrust because the same piece is moved twice before all the others are moved at least once). In both instances, a rigid approach leads to 4. Nc3, whose chief virtue is that it develops a piece toward the center. But because the variation is popular, we might as well review it despite its limitations.

The first diagramed position is symmetrical, White's sole advantage being the first move. With his c-pawn blocked, White has insufficient support for the immediate 5. d4. The center therefore remains closed, at least for a while, and play proceeds slowly. It's easy to go astray without open lines for attack, which explains why the line is often played without a plan.

Although early castling is not always disastrous, one should be careful about doing it too soon. For example, 5. 0-0 is fine, though it somewhat cedes the initiative and unnecessarily tips White's hand. More flexible is 5. d3, a useful move that reveals little, for Black can't automatically assume White is going to castle Kingside. An example of premature castling and its attendant pitfalls is the game Dubois-Steinitz, from their 1862 match (Diagram 2):

1. e4 e5 2. Nf3 Nc6 3. Bc4 Bc5 4. 0-0 Nf6 5. d3 d6 6. Bg5

DIAGRAM 2

With Black still able to castle Queenside, the Bishop pin doesn't work, for Black can risk a Kingside pawn storm.

6 ... h6 7. Bh4 g5 8. Bg3 h5 9. h4 Bg4 10. c3 Qd7 11. d4 exd4 12. e5 dxe5 13. Bxe5 Nxe5 14. Nxe5 Qf5 15. Nxg4 hxg4 16. Bd3 Qd5 17. b4

0-0-0 18. c4 Qc6 19. bxc5 Rxh4 20.f3 Rdh8 21. fxg4 Qe8 22. Qe2 Qe3+ 23. Qxe3 dxe3 24. g3 Rh1+ 25. Kg2 R8h2+ 26. Kf3 Rxf1+ 27. Bxf1 Rf2+ 28. Kxe3 Rxf1
And Black won.

If, after 1. e4 e5 2. Nf3 Nc6 3. Nc3 Nf6 4. Bc4 Bc5, White plays 5.d3, Black should continue 5 ... d6, protecting his KP and opening a path for his QB. Less prudent is 5 ... 0-0, when 6. Bg5 presents pesky threats. If then 6 ... d6, the thematic 7.Nd5 will disrupt Black's Kingside (Diagram 3):

DIAGRAM 3

A common mistake in such positions is to attack the Bishop (7 ... h6). This simply loses a pawn (8. Nxf6+ gxf6 9. Bxh6) and leaves Black in a hopeless situation. Among the dangers he must watch for is an invading Queen on g7. A game won by seven-year-old Josh Waitzkin at the Manhattan Chess Club Friday Night Rapids shows what can happen if Black continues carelessly: 9 ... Re8 10. 0-0 Be6 11. Nh4 Ne7? 12. Bxe6 fxe6 13.Qg4+, and White mates.

If Black castles prematurely (l. e4 e5 2. Nf3 Nc6 3. Bc4 Bc5 4. Nc3 Nf6 5. d3 0-0), he can avoid most of the sting of 6. Bg5 by the time-wasting 6 ... Be7. If instead he tries to drive off the Bishop by 6 ... h6, he might run into 7.h4, a typical sacrifice in this type of position. Black shouldn't take the Bishop, at least not immediately, for the opening of the h-file here spells curtains. An illustrative variation: 7 ... hxg5 8. hxg5 Ng4 9. g6 Nxf2 10. Nxe5 (threatening 11. Rh8+ Kxh8 12. Qh5+ Kg8 13. Qh7 mate) 10 ... Nxd1 11. Bxf7+ Rxf7 12. gxf7+ Kf8 13. Rh8+ Ke7 14. Nd5+ Ke6 (not 14 ... Kd6 when 15. Rxd8 Kxe5 16. Re8+ Kd4 17. Rxd1 threatens both 18. c3 mate and 18. f8 = Q) 15. Re8+ and 16. f8 = Q when White wins easily.

If Black hasn't castled he can usually play h6 without trouble, as in 1. e4 e5 2. Nf3 Nc6 3. Bc4 Bc5 4. Nc3 Nf6 5. d3 d6 6. Bg5 h6. After 7. Bxf6 (7. Bh4 can be safely answered by 7 ... g5) 7 ... Qxf6 8. Nd5

Qd8 White's edge is minimal. Another way to deal with the threat of 7. Nd5 in the above line is 6 ... Be6 (Diagram 4):

DIAGRAM 4

If White now continues 7. Nd5, Black's game is all right after 7 ... Bxd5 8. Bxd5 h6 9. Bh4 (or 9. Bxf6 Qxf6) 9 ... g5 10. Bg3 Nxd5. One thing White shouldn't play in the above position is 7. Bxe6. Although 7 ... fxe6 creates doubled pawns, the exchange actually strengthens Black's game. He then has control of the center (the pawn at e6 is an asset, not a liability) and an open f-file for attack, especially after castling. Furthermore, his Queen could readily participate in the attack, shifting from d8 to e8 to g6 or h5. Generally speaking, don't exchange Bishops on your opponent's K3 square in similar situations. You'll give him doubled pawns but get an inferior game.

When played correctly, this opening doesn't give White very much, and that's why it's almost never seen in serious tournaments. But teachers encourage beginners to play it because it's easy to learn (and to teach) and because it introduces, at least in a rudimentary fashion, the most basic principles of development. If you're going to play it, study it first. Don't play it mechanically. And if you want to improve your chess, don't be afraid to move on to something else.

The Ruy Lopez, anyone?

TRANSPOSITION

There Are Times When Playing Moves in Reverse Order Can Still Get You Where You Want to Be

Transposition is one of the chess world's most mystical-sounding terms. Yet, it is actually one of the simplest to understand. In most openings, you reach a certain position by playing an accepted order of moves. If you reach that position by playing those same moves, but in a different order, you have transposed moves. The position achieved (and the process itself) is called a transposition.

Diagram 1: This Queen's Gambit position is ordinarily reached by the direct route, 1. d4 d5 2. c4 e6. But the indirect path, 1. c4 e6 2. d4 d5, is an equally effective transposition.

DIAGRAM 1

You might transpose moves in order to sidestep an inferior line, lure your opponent into a trap or bad game, transfer the opening from one you don't like to one you do, exploit inaccurate play, or simply because you've changed your mind.

Transpositions are mainly important to opening theory, but they can significantly affect the middlegame and endgame too. Surprising combinations can be overlooked, in fact, because a player considers proper moves in the wrong sequence. It may be necessary to transpose the move order to discover the winning line. In Diagram 2, Black might naturally analyze 1 ... Ng4 followed by 2 ... Qxh2. This approach is too slow, giving White time to organize a defense (say, with 2. Qf4). But Black can succeed by reversing the move order, transposing the moves in his analytic sequence. The tactic works if he plays 1 ... Qxh2 + and follows with 2 ... Ng4 + .

DIAGRAM 2

BLACK TO MOVE

Many seemingly unimportant transpositions actually obscure subtle points. White, for example, could start the game with either g3 or Nf3, but only 1. Nf3 stops Black's reply 1 ... e5.

Moves are often transposed to avoid particular responses. After I. d4, suppose Black wanted to respond with the Dutch Defense (1 ... f5) but elude the Staunton Gambit (2. e4). He might camouflage his plans by first playing 1 ... e6. If 2. c4, then he could set up the Dutch with 2 ... f5. The opener 1 ... e6 is also more flexible than 1 ... f5, for it doesn't reveal as much about Black's defensive strategy. Instead of a Dutch, the game could easily become a normal Queen's Gambit (2. c4 d5), a Nimzo-Indian Defense (2. c4 Nf6 3. Nc3 Bb4), a Queen's Indian Defense (2. c4 Nf6 3. Nf3 b6), a Benoni Defense (2. c4 c5) and so on. Here we see how skillful transposition can help a player disguise his true intentions.

By playing so noncommittally, however, Black must be prepared if his opponent also engineers a transposition. After 1. d4 e6, White could change the game's character completely with 2. e4, switching from a QP opening to a KP one! This explains why some players (former world champion Mikhail Botvinnik included) were expert at both the Dutch and French defenses. It also suggests that to understand a specific opening you may have to verse yourself in others, no matter how dissimilar, that might come about through transposition.

Another approach is to try for the same general setup against everything. The problem here is that it encourages mechanical moving. Some players make the same five moves of the King's Indian Attack (1. Nf3, 2. g3, 3. Bg2, 4. 0-0, 5. d3—though not

necessarily in this order) regardless of what their opponents do.
The variation 1. Nf3 d5 2. g3 Nf6 3. Bg2 e6 4. 0-0 Be7 5. d3 0-0 6. Nbd2
c5 7. e4 Nc6 8. e5 Nd7 9. Re1 (Diagram 3) is ripe for transposition.
The same position can also be reached from a French Defense (1. e4
e6 2. d3 Nf6 3. Nd2 c5 4. Ngh3 Nc6 5. g3 d5 6. Bg2 Be7 7. 0-0 0-0 8. e5
Nd7 9. Re1) as well as from a Sicilian Defense (1. e4 c5 2. Nf3 e6 3. d3
Nc6 4. g3 d5 5. Nbd2 Nf6 6. Bg2 Be7 7. 0-0 0-0 8. e5 Nd7 9. Re1).

DIAGRAM 3

Deeper and more intricate transpositions can develop quite de-
ceptively. Variations that seem to differ totally may lead to highly
similar positions. Two such positions may be considered transpositions if their essential characteristics are the same. A remarkable
example of this type of transposition occurred in the 21st and final
game for the 1972 world championship in Reykjavik, Iceland, between Boris Spassky and Bobby Fischer. With Spassky's help,
Fischer as Black took a sharp variation of the Sicilian Defense (**1. e4
c5 2. Nf3 e6 3. d4 cxd4 4. Nxd4 a6 5. Nc3 Nc6 6. Be3 Nf6 7. Bd3 d5
8. exd5 exd5 9. 0-0 Bd6 10. Nxc6 bxc6 11. Bd4 0-0 12. Qf3,** the actual
moves of the game—see Diagram 4) and subtly transformed it into
what looks like a drawish Scotch Game (1. e4 e5 2. Nf3 Nc6 3. d4
exd4 4. Nxd4 Nf6 5. Nc3 Bb4 6. Nxc6 bxc6 7. Bd3 d5 8. exd5 cxd5
9. 0-0 0-0 10. Bg5 c6 11. Qf3 Bd6, a strikingly similar transposition—
Diagram 5).

DIAGRAM 4

DIAGRAM 5

The resulting positions differ in small ways but are essentially alike. Why did Fischer do it? Certainly he did not fear the Sicilian position, for he is an expert in that defense. Yet Fischer, an inveterate KP player until his match with Spassky, was even more comfortable in the Scotch-type of position. By easing Spassky out of his chosen field and onto his own turf, Fischer took some of the fire out of Spassky's plan.

Herein lies the greatest benefit of learning to recognize and use transpositions. Most players, even top grandmasters, are most at home in certain types of positions. But you can't always count on being able to achieve your favorite setting from any particular opening scheme. You can, however, enhance your chances of finding yourself in friendly waters if you learn to search for and steer for favorable transpositions.

Skill in employing transpositions, as with many facets of chess, depends on recognizing patterns. Consistently analyzing and classifying positions develops the facility. When examining a position, try to recall another example like it. Ask relevant questions. How similar are the two situations? If they differ, are the differences significant? Doing this should cultivate needed skills and prepare you for higher levels of play. It even makes the game more fun.

3

TACTICS

PIN 'EM! FORK 'EM!

Use These Five Evil Tricks to Bring Your Opponents to Their Knees

Chess," said the German master Richard Teichmann (1868–1925), "is ninety-nine percent tactics." Although this absurdly leaves only one percent for strategy—and everything else—Teichmann was right to emphasize the importance of tactical play. All your careful strategic planning can be ruined by one tactical shot.

Strategy and tactics are related concepts, working hand in hand. A *strategy* is a plan that involves general thinking, and it usually takes several moves to complete. *Tactics* are short-range operations that often make up part of a strategy. Tactics seldom involve more than a few specific, precise moves.

There are two general classes of tactics: mating and nonmating. The first, of course, leads to checkmate, the second to a gain of material. Nonmating tactics are mainly based on double attacks—one move that presents your opponent with two problems at once. Here are the five basic types:

1. Forks

A *fork* occurs when you attack two or more enemy units with the same move. Diagram 1 shows examples of White pieces forking Black ones.

A fork succeeds if the enemy cannot save both men. Sometimes both attacked men can be saved if one can be moved away so that it can protect the other attacked man, or it creates a counterthreat that must be parried, thus gaining time to save the other man.

In position A, the fork is unsuccessful; Black can check with his Rook and then move his Knight to safety. Even if the White King had been a Knight, Black could still save the day with 1 ... Ra5 or 1 ... Rd6. Then, after 2. Bxc8 Rxd5, material is still even.

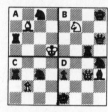   

DIAGRAM 1   DIAGRAM 2

In position C, White's fork is successful. Even though Black can move the Rook to protect the Knight, the trade of pawn for Knight is in White's favor.

The most effective forks usually involve checks; the threat to the King prevents your opponent from using a saving counterattack. In positions B and D, Black must move out of check, and once he does White will have his choice of goodies.

2. Pins

A *pin* prevents or discourages an enemy piece from moving, because to do so would expose a more valuable piece or a key square to attack. Diagram 2 shows examples.

Position A illustrates an *absolute pin*. The Bishop pins the Knight to the King. It is an absolute pin because the Knight can't move.

Position B shows a *relative pin*. The pinned piece, the Bishop, can move to e4 with check. Once White gets out of check, Black can save the Rook.

The virtue of most pins is that they immobilize the pinned man. If you cannot win a pinned man immediately, you can sometimes attack it again and again until it becomes indefensible. Often, you can win a pinned piece by merely attacking it with a pawn. In position A, White to play wins Black's Knight with 1. c4.

3. Skewers

A *skewer* looks like a pin in reverse. Diagram 3 shows two examples.

The basic difference between a pin and skewer is that, in skewers, the second of the two enemy men being attacked is never more valuable than the first (otherwise, you have a pin).

In position A, the bishop skewers the King and Knight. The Bishop forces the King out of the way and captures the Knight. (If

DIAGRAM 3

DIAGRAM 4

the positions of King and Knight were reversed, we would have a pin.) It would also be a skewer if Black's King were a Rook. But, in that case, Black could move 1 ... Rc8 or 1 ... Re6, protecting the Knight.

In position B, Black's two Bishops are skewered, and there is nothing he can do to avoid losing one of them.

4. Undermining

Undermining occurs when an opposing man's protection is removed or driven away. It takes several forms and is sometimes called *removing the defender or exploiting an overworked man.* Diagram 4 illustrates the concept.

In position A, White wins a piece—not by capturing immediately on d5, but by taking first on b6. This undermines the support of Black's Bishop, and White comes out a piece ahead.

In position B, White notices that Black's pawn at f6 is overworked—it must protect both the pawn at e5 and Knight at g5. Thus: 1. Bxe5 fxe5 2. Qxg5, and White has won a pawn.

DIAGRAM 5   DIAGRAM 6

5. Discovered Attacks

A *discovered attack* (or *discovery*) occurs when you move one man so that it uncovers another of your men's firepower against an enemy man (See diagram 5).

Although the stationary man gives the discovered attack, often the moving man delivers an attack as well. In position A, White plays 1. Nc5, simultaneously attacking the bishop at b7 and unleashing his Bishop against Black's Knight at c4. Black loses a piece. Notice that Black could save the day if he didn't have a pawn at a5 with 1 ... Na5, moving one attacked piece to protect another—a common saving tactic.

When the stationary piece unleashes a direct attack to the enemy King, the tactic is called *discovered check*. In such situations, the moving attacker virtually can take or threaten with impunity, because the enemy must get out of check first. In position B, White can play 1. Bxf5, a move that would normally lose the Bishop. But in this case Black is in check from White's Rook. White will capture Black's Queen on the next move. Devastating!

When both the moving and stationary men give check, this is called *double check*. Becuse the only way to deal with two checks at once is to move the King, double checks can produce deadly results, even when both attacking men could individually be captured. In Diagram 6, White mates with 1. Nf6, even though both the Queen and Knight would be taken separately.

One final important piece of advice: *Chess is a two-way game.* As you search for tactics, don't forget that your opponent is doing the same thing. So, for both attack and defense, stay sharp, keep alert, concentrate, and watch your game improve.

YOU CAN DO IT

Practice These Important Techniques to Sharpen Your Tactical Play

Last time, we defined and described five basic tactics—forks, pins, skewers, discovered attacks, and undermining. You weren't shown how to integrate these weapons into your own arsenal, however, or how to sharpen your overall tactical skills. Master and teachers tend to differ in their recommendations, so there's no standard way to improve your strength in this area. Nevertheless, some of the following tips may prove helpful.

• *Know the squares.* Learn to appreciate the way squares link up vertically, horizontally, and diagonally. Color can be important, for it easily suggests diagonal lines of force. The dark color of e7, for example, may suggest an attack from a3, a square available to White's Queen Bishop. Likewise, think of specific squares as corresponding with ranks and files. The square e7, for example, can be attacked from the seventh rank and e-file (or King-file). Practice by closing your eyes and visualizing an empty chessboard. Choose a starting point and go from square to square, identifying colors, connective routes, square names, and so on. Do this often and you should naturally imagine converging lines of attack in your own games.

• *Think in patterns and themes.* Notice how pieces work together (how, for example, a White Bishop on d3 often combines with the Queen on c2 to attack the enemy's h-pawn—or turn the pieces around and you may have a powerful mating threat if Black has castled Kingside). You can add to your knowledge of these concepts by studying textbooks that group related ideas, proceeding step by step from simple themes to harder ones. A few of the better works are *The Art of the Checkmate* by Renaud and Kahn, *The Basis of Combination in Chess* by Dumont, *Simple Checkmates* by Gilliam, and *Tal's Winning Chess Combinations* by Tal and Khenkin. I recommend these books because they are organized manuals and not mere compilations of random problems (although such can be useful, as we shall see).

• *Classify.* When you come upon a tactical idea, relate it to others you've seen. Also try to make analogies. Ask questions such as "How is this situation similar to others?" You may want to create your own catalog of tactics. In filing these positions, give them descriptive names so they will be easier to remember.

• *Regularly solve problems.* To stay sharp, it's important to think tactically on a daily basis. A good method is to work with books of tactical problems. These collections should differ from the previously mentioned instructional manuals. They should instead contain random, but practical, examples. Working with uncataloged positions helps you simulate game conditions. After all, in your own contests, there won't be a genie standing by to alert you to the presence of a mate in three. Two good books for this type of training are Fred Reinfeld's *1001 Checkmates* and his *1001 Chess Combinations and Sacrifices.* Try to solve these problems within a certain time limit, thereby creating pressures similar to those in real games. This also develops your ability to calculate quickly and efficiently, which is necessary for tactical play.

• *Do it in your head.* Whether solving problems or playing over variations, get into the habit of analyzing without moving the pieces. Force yourself to do this no matter how hard it seems, even if you can see only a move or two ahead. If you're having trouble visualizing your analysis, instead of moving the pieces, use your fingers as guideposts, pointing them to the imagined squares (but do this only when studying—never in a real game!). It may also help to say the moves aloud or write them down as you practice. Gradually, you will no longer need these crutches, being fully able to retain entire games in your head. Blindfold play can develop these skills.

• *Play sharp openings.* You will be better able to handle tactical situations if you constantly immerse yourself in them. It therefore makes sense to play gambits and aggressive opening systems. This may cause you to lose some games, but it should eventually accomplish its aim: to make you more comfortable with tactical positions. Later on, you can always change your opening repertoire to suit your style or to widen your knowledge of the game.

• *Play speed chess.* This suggestion has its drawbacks, so follow it with caution. Too much blitz, especially before playing a serious game, can lead to blunders and carelessness. It also tends to promote superficial thinking. On the other hand, by its very nature, speed chess is more tactical. Quick, short-range threats are about all one can conceive of under time pressure, so practicing this way usually cultivates a feeling for tactics.

• *Study the games of attacking players.* This idea hardly needs explanation. While almost all top players are masters of tactics, some have styles particularly conducive to tactical confrontations. A few examples are Mikhail Tal, Alexander Alekhine, Frank Marshall, and Rudolf Spielmann.

• *Analyze complicated positions.* Do it in your head, time yourself, and keep notes. The more complicated, the better—though such problems can be tackled only after you've already acquired some tactical skills. After you've studied a position for thirty minutes and written down your analysis, compare your ideas with the suggested solution. As you do this again and again, you will find yourself analyzing more efficiently, writing down lengthier variations, and coming closer to the actual answers. Alexander Kotov claimed he practically became a grandmaster just by virtue of doing this.

The above suggestions apply specifically to developing your tactical skills. They have little to do with over the board play, so here are a few pointers to help you during actual games.

• *Look for double attacks.* Notice when opposing pieces are lined up or connect to the same square.

• *Exploit pins.* If you already are pinning an enemy man, search for a way to attack it again, especially with a pawn.

• *Get the most from your attacks.* For example, when giving a discovered attack, make sure the moving man does as much damage as possible.

• *Carefully evaluate captures and exchanges.* Before trading off an enemy piece, first see if its protection can be removed or driven away.

• *Try to foresee tactics.* In calm positions, post your men to give them the best opportunities for tactical play.

Perhaps you have your own ideas on the subject, and they've proved valuable to you. If so, drop us a line and let us know what they are. We're always looking for good suggestions.

OF ROOKS AND HARD PLACES

With Two-Rook Mates, It Is Better (and Less Embarrassing) to Give Than to Receive

The two-Rook mate is one of the very first mating patterns that a beginning player encounters. Also known as the linear mate, it is usually formed when one Rook checks along an outside row, while the other Rook guards the next row in from the edge. The defending King is thus trapped as in Diagrams 1a and 1b. This same mate would also result if one of the Rooks were replaced by a Queen as in Diagram 1c (Morphy-Amateur, New Orleans 1858). Morphy delivered an immediate mate with **1. 0-0!** But other examples in this article will focus on linear, two-Rook mates without the Queen.

Another simple, linear mate occurred in the game Edward Lasker-Sir George Thomas (London 1912). In Diagram 2, White concluded a famous combination with the discovered mate, **1. Rh2 + Kg1 2. Kd2 mate!** Lasker might also have played 2. 0-0-0 mate—the same mate-by-castling idea as in Diagram 1c.

If two-Rook mates were as simple as those in the first two diagrams, there would be little need to write about them at all. The beginning player would, presumably, master them himself within his first dozen games or so. The difficulty with this mate is that it usually occurs as the result of a preliminary tactic involving a sacrifice or, say, the deflection theme. The following five diagrams will

DIAGRAM 1A–1C: TWO-ROOK MATES   DIAGRAM 2: WHITE TO MOVE

help to familiarize readers with some of the tricks leading to linear mates and with some of the common settings for these mates. But do not kid yourself: if even the strongest players fail to play these mates or, as we shall see, fall into them, then the learning process occasionally will be painful.

There is a slightly more complex situation in Diagram 3 from the game Aronin–Chekhover (USSR 1949). The White player, an international master, overlooked 1. Qxe6+, sacrificing the Queen to deflect Black's Rook from the defense of g7. After 1 ... Rxe6, White ends it with 2. Rg7+ Kh8 3. Rxf8 mate. Take a look at Diagrams 1a and 1b to see the identical type of pattern.

In Diagram 4 (Goglidze-Botvinnik, Moscow 1935), the White King looks safely tucked away, castled and shielded behind a Rook. But in reality, White's first two ranks are quite vulnerable. Botvinnik swept aside the protective wall with the explosive Queen sacrifice, 1 ... Qxf1+. After 2. Kxf1 Rb1 + 3. Ke2, Black would mate with 3 ... Rc2. The pattern works here because Black's pawn at e4 prevents White's King from reaching the third rank. This means that the second rank functions as an outside row as in Diagrams 1a and 1b.

DIAGRAM 3: WHITE TO MOVE

DIAGRAM 4: BLACK TO MOVE

It's appropriate that Hollywood, California, was the scene of one of the showiest two-Rook mates (see Diagram 5). In the 1931 blindfold simultaneous game Alekhine-Borochow, the world champion Alekhine set up a linear mate on the outside files with a nice line-clearing Queen sacrifice—a common tactic in this type of mate. It was, in fact, the move before the Queen sacrifice which showed Alekhine's genius. The obvious 1. Rh3, threatening mate at h7, can be met by 1 ... Bf5, when 2. Nxf5 is answered by 2 ... Qxf5. Instead, Alekhine cleared the g-file with 1. Ne6!, which compelled Black's resignation. If Black had continued 1 ... Bxe6 (what else?), White sacrifices his Queen to force a vertical, linear mate: 2. Qxh7+ Kxh7

DIAGRAM 5: WHITE TO MOVE

DIAGRAM 6: WHITE TO MOVE

DIAGRAM 7: WHITE TO MOVE

3. Rh3+ Bh4 4. Rhxh4 mate. Of course, this type of sacrifice and mate works just as well on ranks as on files.

The game Polugaevsky-Szilagyi (Moscow 1960) provides a more complicated example of the vertical, two-Rook mate. In Diagram 6, GM Polugaevsky played **1. Rg1+**, which then forced **1 ... Kh6**, since 1 ... Kh5 allows 2. Rxh7 mate. The first point to remember about this position is that Black's King is tied down to guarding h7. The second point to think about is that Black's King is so poorly placed that there just *must* be a two-Rook mate. But how can White maneuver his Rook from d7 to the open h-file? He cannot play 2. Rd3 because of the obvious 2 ... Rxd3, and the Black King covers the potential mating square at h7. The answer is to divert Black's Rook out of position with the deflection sacrifice **2. Bf8+!** After the forced response **2 ... Rxf8** (don't forget that 2 ... Kh5 is suicide after 3. Rxh7 mate), White has the time to play the deadly **3. Rd3.** Mate with Rh3 is now unavoidable.

It will surprise no one that the former world champion, Anatoly Karpov, also knows a bit about the linear mate. In Diagram 7 from Karpov-Mecking (Hastings 1973–74), the world champion faces a neat little problem: how can he mate the Black King when it is not trapped on the board's edge? Karpov realized that the web of Black and White pawns in conjunction with his well-placed King permitted a vertical, linear mate with **1. Rg7**, threatening 2. Rf3 mate.

The moral here is a democratic one: even the great nabobs of our game—the IMs and GMs—fall into two-Rook mates. Mates which are, forgive me, meant for rookies.

MATING LESSONS

Back Rank Mates Are Facts of Life—It's Time to Learn About Them

This article is the first of five lessons on middlegame mating patterns. Among the patterns that we will cover are smothered, Arabian, crisscross, and epaulet mates. The most familiar pattern is, arguably, the back rank mate, which is the subject of this lesson.

DIAGRAM 1A–1D: BACK RANK MATES

DIAGRAM 2A–2C: BACK RANK MATES

Back rank mates occur when a Rook or Queen checks a trapped King along the eighth rank. Such mates often snare beginners who either leave their back rank unguarded, while denying their King an escape square (Diagram 1a), or who forget that an apparent escape square is actually controlled by the opponent (Diagrams 1b, 1c, and

1d). Then again, the back rank may be defended—but insufficiently. In Diagram 2a, White mates by 1. Rd8+ Rxd8 2. Rxd8.

In other instances, the back rank may seem to be adequately defended, but its protection can be reduced by a sacrifice. In Diagram 2b, Black finishes with 1 ... Qxf1+ 2. Rxf1 Rd1+ 3. Rxd1 Rxd1 mate. Finally, a defender may simply be pinned into a mating position (Diagram 2c).

Three Back Rank Themes

Many back rank threats win material rather than force mate when a defending piece is forced to do too many things. Three common winning themes are (1) Reducing the number of defenders (as in 2b); (2) Deflecting a defending piece from its proper position; and (3) Driving the King to a bad square.

In Diagram 3 from Bernstein-Capablanca (Moscow 1914), we have a classic example of deflection. Capablanca concluded matters with the stunning 1 ... Qb2!! The Black Queen is, of course, immune: 2. Qxb2 Rd1 mate. White's real problem is that he can move neither his Rook nor Queen without losing immediately: I. 2. Rc2 Qb1+ 3. Qf1 Qxc2, followed by the crushing 4 ... Rd1. II. 2. Qe1 Qxc3! 3. Qxc3 Rd1+, and Black mates next move.

DIAGRAM 3: BLACK TO MOVE   DIAGRAM 4: BLACK TO MOVE

A variation on this theme occurred in the game Lowtzky-Tartakower (Jurata 1937). Tartakower skewered White with 1 ... Qd2! (Diagram 4)

White must now lose his Rook because if 2. Qxd2 Rf1 mate. In a phrase, White cannot save his Rook while continuing to guard against the potential mate at f1.

The most famous example of deflection comes from a possibly apocryphal game, Adams-Torre (New Orleans 1925?). As shown here (Diagram 5), Black's Rook at e8 is both attacked and guarded twice. White's brilliant series of Queen offers destroys this balance. The game concluded: **1. Qg4! Qb5** (if 1 ... Qxg4, White forces mate with 2. Rxe8 + ; and if 1 ... Qd8, White can weaken Black's back rank with 2. Qxc8!—the same basic idea as in diagram 2b) **2. Qc4!! Qd7** (once again, if either 2 ... Qxc4 or 2 ... Rxc4, White finishes with 3. Rxe8 +) **3. Qc7!!** (the White Queen is still immune from capture) **3 ... Qb5 4. a4! Qxa4 5. Rc4! Qb5** (Black could surrender his Queen for a mere Rook after 5 ... Qxe4 6. Rxe4, but he cannot try 5 ... Rxe4 because of 6. Qxc8 + , forcing mate) **6. Qxb7!!** and **Black resigned.** White wins a whole Queen.

In Diagram 6 (Mileika-Voitkevich, Riga 1963), there is a surprising variation on the previous theme. Doesn't a back rank mate seem impossible in this position?

But White finds a truly amazing line to divert the Black Queen from the d8-square. The trick is **1. Ra7! Qb6 2. Rb7!!**, and Black must lose material because the White Rook cannot be captured without allowing mate at d8.

DIAGRAM 5: WHITE TO MOVE   DIAGRAM 6: WHITE TO MOVE

In Diagrams 3–6, the superior side won material by deflecting at least one important defensive piece. In Zatulovskaya-Lazarevic, Minorca 1973 (Diagram 7), we see our third theme: forcing the enemy King onto a bad square.

White forces mate with the summary **1. Qf8 +** . If Black should capture with 1 ... Kxf8, Black has the back rank finish 2. Rd8 mate. Of course if 1 ... Kh7, White mates prosaically with 2. Qg7.

This tactic appeared in a much more handsome version in Vidmar-Euwe (Carlsbad 1929).

In Diagram 8, Vidmar played **1. Re8+**. Black came back with **1 ... Bf8** in order to avoid the loss of a Rook after 1 ... Kh7 2. Qd3+. At this point, White drove the Black King to a vulnerable square with **2. Rxf8+ Kxf8**. After **3. Nf5+**, Black tried to flee with **3 ... Kg8** to avoid 5. Rd8 mate—the same mate as in diagram 1c. But he got hit

DIAGRAM 7: WHITE TO MOVE

DIAGRAM 8: WHITE TO MOVE

by the identical idea in Diagram 7 (**4. Qf8+**), when White will mate with either 4. Rd8 or 5. Qg7.

If you are a beginner, then be careful about moving major pieces off your first row when enemy counterparts already occupy open files. Another safety measure is to make room (*Luft*) for your King. On the other hand, don't automatically move the pawns in front of your King's position.

ABCs' KNIGHT-LINE

Smothered Mate Is Like a Fine Diamond: It's Rare, Beautiful and Forever Sparkling

Thank heaven that the Knight can jump over other pieces! Otherwise there would never be the thrill of the ultimate Knight line: smothered mate. Arguably the most memorable of all mating patterns, smothered mate occurs when a Knight checks a King over a cluster of hostile forces. It happens seldom, but even beginners aspire to create its elusive pattern.

In Diagram 1a, there is a typical smothered mate in which the Black King is, yes, smothered behind a wall of its own Rook and pawns, with the White Knight giving mate at c7. The same mating check can also be given at g6, when the beheaded King is surrounded (see Diagram 1b) by his own pieces. In other cases, as in Diagram 1c, the mate is helped along by a pin. The White Queen cannot, of course, capture the Black Knight because of the back rank pin. In Diagram 1d, the same pinning idea also works along files.

The best-known process for arriving at a smothered mate is given in Diagram 2a, an idea referred to as "Philidor's Legacy." (Actually the concept first appeared in Lucena's manuscript of 1497.)

DIAGRAM 1A–1D

DIAGRAM 2A–2D

The basic tactic is two-fold: force the Black Rook to capture White's Queen on b8 and mate with the Knight on Black's c7. One try is to sacrifice the Queen immediately with 1. Qb8+, but Black can simply capture the Queen with his King, thereby avoiding smothering himself. The correct line involves a double discovered check: 1. Nc7+ Kb8 2. Na6++ Ka8 3. Qb8+ Rxb8 4. Nc7 mate.

It helps to remember that Philidor's Legacy cannot always be forced. In Diagram 2b, the Rook can sacrifice itself were White to try Nc7+. There are times when the Black Knight cannot reach the Bishop's square for a check, as in Diagram 2c where the Black Queen occupies the key square. However, in this case White's b1 is already guarded twice by Black's Queen and Bishop, and Black can mate in two: 1 ... Qb1+ 2. Rxb1 (or either Knight takes the Queen), 2 ... Nc2 mate. On other occasions, such as Diagram 2d, the Rook cannot take the Knight when it checks because of a mate on the first rank. Thus, Black mates with either 1 ... Nf2+ 2. Rxf2 Qe1+ 3. Rf1 Qxf1 mate or with 1 ... Nf2+ 2. Kg1 Nh3++ 3. Kh1 Qg1+ 4. Rxg1 Nf2 mate.

There are a large number of sacrificial themes which can aid in implementing smothered mate. In diagram 3a, White can win the Black Queen by playing; but there is a deflection sacrifice which is even stronger, 1. Qxa7+ Qxa7 2. Nc7 mate. The smothered mate still works because Black's a-pawn has been replaced by his Queen. Smothered mate does not always occur in the corner of the board; it may turn up suddenly in the center and even right in the opening! A typical pattern appears in Diagram 3b. Here's how the great Reshevsky fell victim to a central smothering (Reshevsky-Margolit, simultaneous, Israel 1958): **1. d4 Nf6 2. c4 e6 3. Nc3 Bb4 4. e3 c5**

DIAGRAM 3A–3C

5. Ne2 Nc6 6. a3 Qa4 7. Bd2 e5 8. axb4 Nxb4 9. Rxa5?? Nd3 mate. Compare the final position with that in 3b.

A rather common smothered mate can also come about because of a pin along the e-file (see Diagram 3c). The openings are filled with traps demonstrating this motif. In the Giuoco Piano: 1. e4 e5 2. Nf3 Nc6 3. Bc4 Nd4 4. Nxe5 Qg5 5. Nxf7 Qxg2 6. Rf1 Qxe4+ 7. Be2 Nf3 mate. In the Caro-Kann: **1.e4 c6 2.d4 d5 3.Nc3 dxe4 4.Nxe4 Nd7 5.Qe2 Ngf6 6.Nd6 mate.** GM Paul Keres caught at least two different opponents in this latter snare during the 1950s, and Alexander Alekhine once mated a team of six(!) opponents in this line in a simultaneous exhibition.

Smothered mates are rare in tournament play, although possibilities of creating them occur more often than you might imagine. The problem is that amateurs overlook their opportunities and stronger players fight hard to prevent such humiliation. When they do occur in master play, they are usually the result of a master overlooking the obvious in an already ruined position. Thus in

Diagram 4 (Benko-Horowitz, U.S. championship 1968), Black saved his threatened Knight with 1 ... Nc2, overlooking the catastrophic 2. Qg8+ with mate next move.

Some of the most famous smothered mates fail to show up on the board. Instead, they are to be found hiding in the notes. A notable example occurred in the "Game of the Century," played in 1956 between IM Donald Byrne (as White) and a certain 13-year-old kid named Bobby Fischer. In Diagram 5, Fischer found the remarkable **1 ... Be6!!** If White had answered with 2. Bxe6, then Black could smother him with 2 ... Qb5+ 3. Kg1 Ne2+ 4. Kf1 Ng3+ 5. Kg1 Qf1+

DIAGRAM 4: BLACK TO MOVE

DIAGRAM 5: BLACK TO MOVE

6. Rxf1 Ne2 mate. This mate is similar to Philidor's Legacy, since with White's h1 and h2 blocked the g1 square functions as a corner square.

For many players, suffering a smothering is a tragedy. Yet there is a lighter side to the theme, as represented in Diagrams 6 and 7. Diagram 6 is the starting point for a problem created by the Russian master Carl Jaenisch in the mid-19th century; and Diagram 7 is the final position. Here, then, is smothered mate with a vengeance: **1. f3+ gxf3 2. exd3+ cxd3 3. Bf5+ exf5 4. Re6+ dxe6 5. Rd4+ cxd4 6. a8=B+** (it is also possible to play 6. a8=Q+)**6 ... Qd5 7. Bxd5+ exd5 8. Nf6+ gxf6 9. Qe5+ fxe5 10. Ng5 mate.**

Under normal circumstances, the Black King might feel quite safe surrounded by so many pawns. But here?

DIAGRAM 6: WHITE MATES IN TEN

DIAGRAM 7: THE FINAL POSITION

MIDDLE EASTERN SKIRMISH

The Arabian Mate

The Arabian mate is one of the oldest known mating patterns. It probably owes its name to the importance of the Knight in the final position and to its appearance in an early Arab chess manuscript. However, the pattern actually involves both a Knight and a Rook working in tandem, with the Rook administering the final check while the Knight protects both the Rook and one escape square. A typical example can be seen in Diagram 1a where White has the choice of two mirror-image mates. He can play either 1. Rb8, mating on the eighth rank, or 1. Ra7, mating on the seventh.

In Diagram 1b, White can force a classic Arabian mate along the seventh rank with 1. Nf6. Black simply has no defense to 2. Rh7 mate. Former world champion Mikhail Tal offers a humorous parallel to 1b in the following position: **W:Kh1, Ra7, Nd5; B:Kh8, Qa4, Rb8, Rc8, Bb4, Bd1, Nd4, Nh6, Pa6, e4, f3.** In spite of his mighty army, Black can only delay the inevitable after 1. Nf6. White's finisher is, of course, the pellucid 2. Rh7 mate.

Meanwhile, Diagram 1c illustrates that the afflicted monarch need not be in the corner to get mated. In this instance, Black plays 1 ... Qxb2 + 2. Qxb2 Rxb2 mate. Finally, in 1d, there is a position (with colors reversed) based on a 1959 Koltanowski-Halsey game. Kolty forced mate by the deflecting tactic **1 ... Qxh2 +!** If White replies with 2. Rxh2, Black can end it with 2 ... Rxg1 mate.

DIAGRAM 1A–1D: ARABIAN MATES

DIAGRAM 2: WHITE TO MOVE

Among the masters, a preliminary sacrifice often precedes an Arabian finale. In Fine-Dake (Detroit 1933), Reuben Fine broke it open (Diagram 2) with **1. Qxg6 +!** The idea of this sacrifice is elementary: to destroy the key defender of the h7 square. Black decided to call it a day. Otherwise, there would have followed 1 ... hxg6 2. Nf6+ Kh8 3. Rh7 mate.

In the game Tartakower-Schlechter (Vienna 1908), there occurred a more complicated version of the theme in Diagram 1d. Tartakower (see Diagram 3) probably reckoned that after **1 ... Rf2 + 2. Kh1,** Black would not have time for 2 ... Nf3 because his Rook at g8 hangs with a check. But he missed the sly **2 ... Rh2 +!!** White resigned because of 3. Kxh2 Nf3 + 4. Kh1 Rxg1 mate.

Most Arabian mates occur in the corners of the board. But there are exceptions. In Diagram 4, which is a position from the game Holt-Bingamon (West Virginia 1947), an Arabian lurks on the eighth rank in the very center of the board. White is in check, but he does not move his King. Instead, he sacrifices his Queen by **1. Qxf3!** At this point, Black should have settled for the loss of a piece after 1 ... dxe4 2. Qxg4. In the game, he played **1 ... Qxf3,** whereupon White mated with **2. Nf6 + Kd8 3. Re8.**

DIAGRAM 3: BLACK TO MOVE

DIAGRAM 4: WHITE TO MOVE

Although Arabian mates are usually products of the late middlegame or the endgame, they also occur in the opening. The previously mentioned game, Holt-Bingamon, went as follows: **1. e4 e5 2. Nf3 Nc6 3. Bc4 Nf6 4. d4 exd4 5. 0-0 Nxe4 6. Re1 d5 7. Nxd4 Qh4 8. g3 Qf6 9. Nf3 Bg4 10. Nbd2 Nd4 11. Nxe4 Nxf3 + 12. Qxf3 Qxf3 13. Nf6 + Kd8 14. Re8 mate.** And here is a line from the Tarrasch Queen's Gambit: **1. d4 d5 2. c4 e6 3. Nc3 c5 4. cxd5 exd5 5. Nf3 Nc6 6. g3 Bg4 7. Ne5 Nxe5 8. dxe5 d4 9. Ne4 Qd5 10. Bg2 Qxe5 11. Bf4 Qh5 12. 0-0 Bxe2 13. Re1! Bxd1 14. Nf6 + Kd8 15. Re8 mate.**

At this point, take a look again at Diagram 1c because the next example (Alekhine–Asgeirsson, Reykjavik 1931) is quite similar. In the dramatic position shown in Diagram 5, Alekhine played the discombobulating **1. Qf6+!**, whereupon Black surrendered. The finish would have been short and sour for the second player. If Black played 1 ... gxf6, White wins by 2. Rf7 mate, as the Knight protects the Rook and covers the e8 square.

DIAGRAM 5: WHITE TO MOVE

In Diagram 6, an Arabian once again lurks along the 7th rank. At first glance in this position (from Sokolov-Ruzhnikov, Correspondence 1966–67), White's Queen appears in deadly danger. But Sokolov calmly ignored the threatened ... hxg5, playing the discovery **1. Rxb7+!** (1 ... Rf6 2. Nc6+ Ke8 3. Re7+ Kf8 4. Qg7 produces a support mate) Black surrendered rather than face 1 ... hxg5 2. Nc6+ Ke8 3. Re7 mate. The point of the sacrifice was to eliminate the b7 pawn guarding the crucial c6 square.

The final position (Diagram 7) is a 1950 endgame study by the Soviet problemist Vladimir Korolkov. White wants to force the Black Rook at a2 to move, thereby permitting Rxb2 mate. But White must avoid any checks so that Black will not have a chance to relieve the mate threat by moving his Rook at a1. The solution: 1. Kg7! fxg6 (if 1 ... f5, White has 2. Kh6 f4 3. Rg2 f3 4. Rf2 R-moves 5. Rxb2 mate)2. Kh6! (White still hides from the checks) 2 ... g5 3. Kh5 g4 4. Kh4 g3 5. Kxg3 R-moves 6. Rxb2 mate.

DIAGRAM 6: WHITE TO MOVE

DIAGRAM 7: WHITE WINS

In my view, there is something furtive about the Arabian mate. It is redolent of hushed nights, the deadly *kris*, and Byzantine intrigue. It is a mate aptly named.

CAISSA'S* SOUTHERN CROSS

When Two Bishops Crisscross the Enemy King, the Brilliancy Prize Is Not Far Behind

The two-Bishop or crisscross mate is spectacular. The setup involves either two Bishops catching a King in a crossfire or a Queen and Bishop working in a similar tandem. The term "crisscross" seems particularly apt because the light square diagonal of one mating piece crosses the dark-square diagonal of the other piece, forming a pattern of the letter "X."

In Diagram 1a, the light-square Bishop mates from a6 while the Queen controls all other escape squares, including the d6-h8 diagonal, which transverses the a6-c8 diagonal. In diagram 1b, there occurs the classic two-Bishop criss-cross in which the Queen can be replaced because h7 and h8 are already blocked by, respectively, a pawn and a Rook. Finally, in diagram 1c, Black uses a common sacrificial theme to introduce the crisscross: he sacrifices his Queen by 1 ... Qxc3 + 2. bxc3 Ba3 mate. This stratagem is commonly called Boden's Mate, named after the winner of the game Schulten-Boden (London 1853), which appears later here.

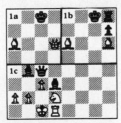

DIAGRAM 1A–1C: CRISSCROSS MATES

DIAGRAM 2: WHITE TO MOVE

*Caissa is the goddess of chess.

An example of the idea given in diagram 1a could have occurred in the game Meek–Morphy (Mobile 1855). White resigned in the position (see Diagram 2), but if he had tried to defend by 1. Bxe3, then Black would have meted out mate with 1 ... Qxe3. Notice that it is mate not only because the e-file is covered but also because the g1-e3 and f1-h3 diagonals are controlled by the Queen and Bishop.

For theory hounds, the crisscross mate pops up in opening manuals like raisins in rice pudding. Here's an embarrassment from the Caro-Kann Defense: 1. e4 c6 2. Nc3 d5 3. d4 dxe4 4. Nxe4 Nf6 5. Nxf6+ exf6 6. Bc4 Be7 7. Qh5 0-0 8. Ne2 g6 9. Qf3 Nd7 10. Bh6 Re8 11. Bxf7+ Kxf7 12. Qb3 mate. Or there's this chess shorty from From's Gambit (Krauthauser-Hermann, Siegen 1934): **1. f4 e5 2. fxe5 d6 3. Nf3 Nc6 4. exd6 Bxd6 5. e4 g5 6. Bb5 g4 7. Bxc6+ bxc6 8. e5 gxf3 9. exd6 Qh4+ 10. Kf1 fxg2+ 11. Kxg2 Bh3+ 12. Kg1 Qd4 mate.**

Crisscross mates often occur as the end product of sacrificial combinations (for example, diagram 1c). The position in Diagram 3 is from the contest Rodzinsky-Alekhine (Moscow 1913). Alekhine loved the pretty point, and with **1 ... Be7!** he scored a beautiful win. The move threatens both 2 ... Rxa8 winning the White Queen and 2 ... Bh4 mate, crisscrossing the White monarch. White, of course, resigned.

As in the aforementioned Schulten-Boden bloodletting (**1. e4 e5 2. Nf3 d6 3. c3 f5 4. Bc4 Nf6 5. d4 fxe4 6. dxe5 exf3 7. exf6 Qxf6 8. gxf3 Nc6 9. f4 Bd7 10. Be3 0-0-0 11. Nd2 Re8 12. Qf3 Bf5 13. 0-0-0 d5 14. Bxd5 Qxc3+ 15. bxc3 Ba3 mate**), the Queen occasionally creates the mating position by sacrificing herself. In Ofstad-Uhlmann (Diagram 4), played at Halle 1963, a little-known Norwegian master humbled GM Uhlmann with a powerful sacrificial sequence. White played the blunt **1. Rxe7,** and Black resigned because of 1 ... Nxe7 2. Qf6+ gxf6 3. Bh6 mate. The important thing to remember is that this flashy combination is really only a variation of Boden's Mate as seen in diagram 1c.

DIAGRAM 3: BLACK TO MOVE

DIAGRAM 4: WHITE TO MOVE

The crisscross also occurs when the King is in the center of the board. In Alekhine–Anon. from a 1925 Paris simultaneous, White delivered Boden's Mate with **1. Qxe6! fxe6 2. Bg6 mate** (see Diagram 5). But don't think that amateurs only are humiliated. Here is Zukertort-Anderssen (Breslau 1865): **1. e4 e5 2. Nf3 Nc6 3. Bb5 Nge7 4. c3 d6 5. d4 Bd7 6. 0-0 Ng6 7. Ng5 h6 8. Nxf7 Kxf7 9. Bc4 + Ke7 10. Qh5 Qe8 11. Qg5 +** (the less fancy **11. Bg5 +** also does the job) **11 ... hxg5 12. Bxg5 mate.**

Nor are such drastic crisscross mates a malady of the lightweight defensive days of the 19th century. In the Diagram 6 game Bolbochan-Pachman (Moscow 1956), White ended the game pronto with the explosive **1. Qxf7 + !!** If Black tries the prosaic 1 ... Kh8, it's over after **2. Qg7 mate.** And if he tries 1 ... Kxf7, there is the crisscrossing **2. Bxe6 mate.**

One of the most spectacular crisscross mates (Diagram 7) occurred in Steinitz-Belaiev (London 1866), when the "Austrian Morphy" terminated the affair with the deflection sacrifice, **1. Qxg8 +**. After 1 ... Qxg8, Steinitz delivered a true right cross with **2. Bh4 +**, with mate next move.

In my own practice, I let loose with a crisscross from the well-trodden Riga Variation of the Ruy Lopez: **1. e4 e5 2. Nf3 Nc6 3. Bb5**

DIAGRAM 5: WHITE TO MOVE

DIAGRAM 6: WHITE TO MOVE

DIAGRAM 7: WHITE TO MOVE

a6 4. Ba4 Nf6 5. 0-0 Nxe4 6. d4 exd4 7. Re1 d5 8. Nxd4 Bd6 9. Nxc6 Bxh2+ 10. Kh1 Qh4 11. Rxe4+ dxe4 12. Qd8+ Qxd8 13. Nxd8+ Kxd8 14. Kxh2. My opponent played 14. ... f5??, allowing 15. Bg5 mate. A week later, in a rapids tournament, I had the same position against the same opponent. Instinctively, he reached to play ... f5??, but caught himself in time, playing instead ... f6.

Had I scored with a second crisscross mate, my friend might justifiably have accused me of a doublecross.

THE MILITANT MATE

Keep a Sharp Eye Out for Epaulet Patterns

The word "epaulet" designates an ornamental decoration worn on both shoulders of military and other uniforms. In chess it refers to the field marshal of mates—a situation in which the victimized King is blocked on its immediate right and left by its own men. Some typical themes can be seen in Diagram 1a–1e. In Diagram 1a, we have the classic setup: the Black King is flanked on either side by obstructing Rooks while the White Queen proves herself to be a tough lady indeed by delivering the mate.

Diagram 1b reveals that the mated King need not occupy an outer row as long as the other escape squares are barricaded or guarded, while diagram 1e demonstrates that other pieces than the Queen can deliver an epaulet mate. The remaining diagram portions, 1c and 1d, will be discussed later.

DIAGRAM 1A–1E: EPAULET MATES

DIAGRAM 2: WHITE TO MOVE

In Diagram 2, from a game played in New York in 1857, Paul Morphy illustrated in classical fashion the motif of 1a. As White against an amateur, Morphy finished by **1. Rf8 + Qxf8 2. Rxf8 + Rxf8 3. Qxg6 mate.** While this type of combination appears simple enough, it is easy to overlook. And it pays to know your basic patterns—as, for example, in the next diagram.

In Diagram 3, the same mate occurs along the side of the board. Playing against an amateur in Vienna in 1861, Wilhelm Steinitz relied on a deflective Rook sacrifice, **1. Rd8 + !** After **... Qxd8 2. Qe6 + Kh7,** he crowned his play with a second Rook sacrifice, **3. Rxh6 + ! gxh6 4. Qf7 mate.** This is a combination that most players would see only if they knew their patterns.

On the subject of patterns, many chess teachers adopt a lofty, if somewhat embarrassed silence. These teachers desire instead to impart "concepts" to their students. After all, requiring pupils to hover over combinations for hours could discourage newcomers to the game. Yet there is simply no shortcut to learning how to play chess with ease and assurance. Sad but true, young players must labor hard to master the basic patterns.

As for epaulets, do they ever occur in the opening? Rarely. But when they do, they usually look like Diagram 1b. One short example begins (and ends) with **1. e4 e5 2. Oh5? Ke7?? 3. Qe5 mate.** Tal calls this "a tragicomic sequence that could put a smile on everyone's face." Perhaps, but what about the loser? Here is another dubious game of uncertain parentage and legitimacy: **1. e4 d5 2. exd5 Qxd5 3. Ke2?? Qe4 mate.** The regnant myth holds 3. Ke2?? to be a *fingerfehler* (a blunder one is forced to play because of having touched a piece by accident).

The conclusion of the game in Diagram 4, Korchnoi-Petersen (Kiev 1964), is an epaulet mate along the lines of Diagram 1e. Pe-

DIAGRAM 3: WHITE TO MOVE

DIAGRAM 4: WHITE TO MOVE

DIAGRAM 5: WHITE WINS

DIAGRAM 6: BLACK TO MOVE

tersen no doubt hoped to retreat his King to e8—and then beyond. But White hit hard with **1. Qg7+ Ke8 2. Qxe7+!!** Black resigned because of 2 ... Kxe7 3. Rg7+ Ke8 4. Nf6 mate. It's bad form to repeat oneself, but this combination again points up the importance of recognizing patterns—in this case, that shown in diagram 1e.

In Diagram 5, we have the concluding part of a 1912 study by the Russian composer Gleb Nikolayevich Zakhodyakin. White concluded with **1. Kg5! Ng8** (if 1 ... Kg7, White plays 2. Rd7+, winning easily) **2. Rh2+ Kg7 3. Rh7+ Kf8 4. Rf7 mate.** Don't forget to check pattern 1a!

The patterns in diagram 1c and 1d offer modification on the usual epaulet mate. The pieces on the losing side assume the outline of an occasional table (in French, *gueridon*), a formation often referred to as a "swallow's tail." Virtually the same situation as in Diagram 1d occurred in Keres-Fischer (Bled 1959). See for yourself: White:Kd5, Rc4, Pc6; Black:Kf5, Qe5, Pg4. Or there is Diagram 6 (Redeley-Baratey, 1962), where Black concluded quickly with **1 ... Rxc2+! 2. Kxc2 Qc3 mate.** Think of White's King as a swallow's head and his Queen and Rook as wings in flight.

DIAGRAM 7: "SWALLOW'S TAIL"

DIAGRAM 8: BLACK TO MOVE

The swallow's tail (plus the swallow, of course) can fly through just about any chessic window. This includes the opening. In the following line from Philidor's Defense (Diagram 7), Black plays passively and suffers a debacle: **1. e4 e5 2. Nf3 d6 3. Bc4 Be7 4. d4 exd4 5. Nxd4 Nd7? 6. Bxf7+ Kxf7 7. Ne6! Kxe6** (if Black tries 7 ... Qe8, White has 8. Nxc7 Qd8 9. Qd5+ Kf8 10. Ne6+, winning Black's Queen) **8. Qd5+ Kf6 9. Qf5 mate.** In the mating position, the Bishop at e7 and the pawn at g7 serve as the "wings."

The position in Diagram 8 is controversial. The game (Anon.-Pillsbury, Blindfold Simultaneous 1899) ended with an extraordinary mating concept: **1... Qf1+ 2. Bg1 Qf3+!! 3. Bxf3 Bxf3 mate!** In my view the final position is a swallow's tail, with the pieces on g1 and h2 serving as the wings.

I call the epaulet a militant rather than a military mate because while the epaulet is as drastic as war, it never ends in stalemate!

4

POSITION PLAY

PROTECTIONISM

Remember That It's as True for Pawns as It Is for People: They Can Never Go Back Home Again

Nothing can get you into trouble faster than an unwise move in the opening. Moving one or both of your center pawns to speed piece development is a good idea. And occasionally it helps to move a wing pawn; for example, moving a pawn to g3 (or g6 for Black) in order to fianchetto a Bishop to g2 (or g7) is often a good plan. But many times it's a bad idea to move wing pawns. Such moves can

- waste time,
- weaken one's position, and
- expose the King.

The most typical error is an early, unnecessary h3 (or h6 for Black). There are times when this push is important, such as in the Ruy Lopez. After 1. e4 e5 2. Nf3 Nc6 3. Bb5 a6 4. Ba4 Nf6 5. 0-0 Be7

6. Re1 b5 7. Bb3 d6, the move 8. h3 helps White avoid the pin 8 ... Bg4.

But moving the h-pawn often consumes valuable time and weakens the square in front of the g-pawn. A good example is 1. d4 Nf6 2. Nd2 (not a good move, but it helps here to illustrate the point) 2 ... e5 3. dxe5 Ng4 4. h3?? (Diagram 1). White should have played 4. Ngf3, since now Black wins the Queen with 4 ... Ne3!, because 5. fxe3 allows 5 ... Qh4+ and mate next. This sacrifice derives its strength from the abysmal 4. h3??, which severely weakened White's control of g3.

Voluntarily moving both your f- and h-pawns early in a game can be tantamount to suicide. This opens a direct line to the King on the e1-h4 diagonal for White and the e8-h5 diagonal for Black. Consider the Dutch Defense, 1. d4 f5. Black's defense is perfectly playable, though he must be careful not to weaken his position any further. If White tries 2. Bg5, Black shouldn't answer with 2 ... h6?, because this seriously damages his hold over g6. A well-known trap here is 3. Bh4 g5 4. Bg3 f4 5. e3 h5 (still trying to "Noah's Ark" the Bishop) 6. Bd3 Rh6?? 7. Qxh5+!, when White will mate on the next move. Black's sixth move was the only time he developed a piece, and that was a terrible choice.

Once g3 (or g6) has been weakened by moving the h-pawn, all kinds of tactics may be used to draw away the f-pawn and expose the King. For instance, after 1.e4 c6 2.d4 d5 3. Bd3 (not the best move here) 3 ... Nf6? 4. e5 Nfd7 (Diagram 2), White can break through with 5. e6!; Black must accept an inferior position, for 5 ... fxe6 is crushed by 6. Qh5+, when White mates in two by sacrificing either the Queen or Bishop on g6. So, if you must move the h-pawn early on, be vigilant against diversionary threats to the f-pawn.

A recurring reason for moving both the f-and h-pawns is to hold on to captured material; often this "pawn-grabbing" can be severely

DIAGRAM 1: AFTER 4. h3

DIAGRAM 2: AFTER 4 ... Nfd7

DIAGRAM 3: AFTER 4 ...f6

DIAGRAM 4: AFTER 4 ... Nd7

punished. In a famous article published in the early 1960s, Bobby Fischer analyzed 1. e4 e5 2. f4 exf4 3. Nf3 g5 4. Bc4 f6? (Diagram 3). This advance protects the g-pawn, creates a pawn chain, and keeps the Knight out of e5. Unfortunately, it also opens the a2-g8 and e8-h5 diagonals. After 5. Nxg5! (clearing the Queen's path), Black can resign. Mate follows after 5 ... fxg5 6. Qh5+ Ke7 7. Qf7+ Kd6 8. Qd5+ Ke7 9. Qe5. Black loses after having played only eight moves, five with pawns and three with the King. You can't neglect development this much and expect to survive.

Moving the f-pawn in the beginning of a game, even without pushing the h-pawn, can still lead to trouble. Damiano's Defense (1. e4 e5 2. Nf3 f6?) provides an illustration. After 3. Nxe5, Black is in real trouble. An example of the potential difficulties: 3 ... fxe5 4. Qh5+ Ke7 (4 ... g6 5. Qxe5+ and wins material) 5. Qxe5+ Kf7 6. Bc4+ Kg6 7. Qf5+ Kh6 8. d4+ g5 9. h4 Be7 10. hxg5+ Kg7 11. Qf7 mate.

Sometimes, even if you have moved neither the f- nor the h-pawn, your position may be just as vulnerable as if you had. This generally happens when one or two pieces have been poorly developed. A case in point is 1. e4 g6 2. d4 d6 3. Nf3 Bg7 4. Bc4 Nd7? (Diagram 4). This Knight move loses, because it blocks the Bishop's control of e6. By getting rid of the f-pawn, White can exploit the weakness of e6 at once. After 5. Bxf7+ Kxf7, Black is in as much trouble as he would have been had he mistakenly moved the f-pawn on his own. He has no answer to 6. Ng5+, for both 6 ... Ke8 and 6 ... Kf8 allow White to immediately capitalize on the hole at e6 with the winning 7. Ne6. And 6 ... Kf6 7. Qf3 is mate.

The lesson is clear: Do not move wing pawns in the opening unless there is a solid reason for doing so. Sometimes your opening system may require such moves—a fianchetto, for example. And sometimes you must move the h-pawn to drive away a hostile piece, most often a Bishop. But remember then that the pawn move is part of a thoughtful system that has already taken into account any potential weaknesses the pawn move may create. Generally, however, if you have the slightest doubt about moving an f- or h-pawn in the opening, don't. Otherwise, you might fall into the holes you leave behind.

A PAWN'S LOT

Pawns Can Come Down with Two Illnesses That Require Special Treatment

The great French master Andre Danican Philidor (1725–95) said that "pawns are the soul of chess." He understood that pawn structure shapes the character of a position, providing the basis for strategy and planning. If your pawn structure is sound, your pieces should have greater chances to attack. If it is weak, the same pieces may be obstructed or forced into passive roles. Two types of recurrent pawn weaknesses are *isolated pawns* and *doubled pawns*.

Isolated Pawns

The isolated pawn stands alone. There are no friendly pawns on the files next to it. If threatened, it must be moved or protected by a

DIAGRAM 1

piece. It sometimes is confused with a passed pawn, but differs from it in a basic way. A passed pawn's movement cannot be hindered by enemy pawns, while an isolated pawn is always restrained or actually blocked by at least one enemy pawn. In Diagram 1, White's a-pawn is passed and his d-pawn is isolated.

Another problem with an isolated pawn is that the square immediately in front of it cannot be controlled by a friendly pawn, allowing enemy pieces to sit there, safe from attack (this is called a *blockade*). Usually, the best piece for a blockade is a Knight, especially when the Knight itself is solidly protected by a pawn (Rooks, because they are more valuable and therefore more vulnerable to attack by pieces of lesser value, tend to be the worst blockaders). Diagram 2 shows the power of a secure blockading Knight. In that position, White has several winning plans, including the idea of 1. a6, followed by 2. b4 and 3. b5.

DIAGRAM 2: WHITE TO MOVE

A special Jekyll-and-Hyde case is the isolated d-pawn, dubbed an *isolani*. It occurs naturally in a variety of openings, including the Tarrasch Defense to the Queen's Gambit (1. d4 d5 2. c4 e6 3. Nc3 c5) and the Tarrasch French Defense (1. e4 e6 2. d4 d5 3. Nd2 c5). Accepting the isolated d-pawn usually leads to a spatial advantage, inasmuch as it generally occupies the fourth rank while being restrained by an enemy pawn on its third. With a pawn on d4, White also has excellent prospects for Knight outposts at e5 and c5.

If you have an isolated pawn, try to:

- Take advantage of the open lines.
- Guard against crippling blockades.
- Exchange it for a good enemy pawn.
- Avoid piece-trades resulting in lifeless endgames.

If you are playing against an isolated pawn, try to:

• Prevent its advance.
• Control, occupy, and use the square in front of it.
• Attack it (especially if it is restrained).
• Exchange pieces to accentuate its weakness and reduce coun-
  terplay.

Doubled Pawns

Doubled pawns are two pawns belonging to the same side lined
up on the same file. They come about through captures, such as in
the Exchange variation of the Ruy Lopez (1. e4 e5 2. Nf3 Nc6 3. Bb5
a6 4. Bxc6 dxc6) or the Saemisch variation of the Nimzo-Indian
Defense (1. d4 Nf6 2. c4 e6 3. Nc3 Bb4 4. a3 Bxc3+ 5. bxc3). This
type of Bishop-for-Knight swap is the most common way to produce
doubled pawns.

Doubled pawns have several potential drawbacks. Because neither doubled pawn can protect the other, they tend to advance at a
snail's pace; they can move only as far and as fast as the lead pawn.
The exchange that creates the doubled pawns may also create other
problems as well—for example, an isolated pawn (note White's a-
pawn in the above Nimzo-Indian) or a favorable pawn majority for
one's opponent (consider White's four-versus-three Kingside advantage in the above Exchange Lopez after the further 5. d4 exd4
6. Qxd4 Qxd4 7. Nxd4; this Kingside pawn majority will give White
better endgame chances).

The worst kinds of doubled pawns are isolated ones, where
neither of the two can be protected by another pawn. These are
easily blockaded by an opposing piece. But even connected doubled pawns can be held back by a single enemy pawn. In Diagram 3,
Black's d-pawn restrains the complex of d- and doubled c-pawns,
for 1. c4 leads to doubled isolated pawns after 1 ... dxc4 2. dxc4.

DIAGRAM 3

Accepting doubled pawns can have its advantages, too—especially if you can exploit the open lines that will be created. Sometimes the doubling process allows a pawn to influence key squares, making those squares inaccessible to the other side's pieces.

If you have doubled pawns, try to:

- Avoid moving them unless you must or can make a good exchange.
- Activate your pieces along the open lines, especially your Rooks.
- Steer clear of exchanges that reduce your piece-play.

If you are playing against them, try to:

- Restrain their movement.
- Avoid exchanges repairing your opponent's structure.
- Attack the weak pawns and squares.
- Neutralize counterplay by intelligent piece exchanges.
- Mobilize your own pawn majority, if you have one.

It's easy to view isolated and doubled pawns as plagues, and novices generally try to avoid them at all costs. But clearly pawn problems can be offset by compensating advantages in time, space, and dynamics. With the exception of being mated, nothing is automatically bad, especially if it can't be exploited by your opponent. Try not to judge chess concepts absolutely, in separate, disconnected items. Not even an isolated pawn.

QUEEN-PAWN QUIRKS

Isolated Queen-pawns Can Be Pillars of Strength or Lame Ducks—and You Must Know the Difference

To get the most from your favorite openings, you should also study the middlegame and endgame positions likely to arise from them.

Once you have learned the strategies and tactics suitable for these situations, you'll be able to play a game confidently from start to finish—without having to grope for a plan as you go along.

The element that you should give the greatest attention to is pawn structure. More than anything else, pawn structure defines the game's character and the way in which play develops.

Almost all openings have a characteristic middlegame pawn structure, and many have a characteristic endgame structure as well. That explains why experienced players can look at a game in an advanced stage and correctly identify the opening. For example, the Exchange variation of the Ruy Lopez (1. e4 e5 2. Nf3 Nc6 3. Bb5 a6 4. Bxc6 dxc6) leaves its mark in Black's doubled c-pawns and White's four-versus-three Kingside pawn majority (once White has exchanged his d-pawn for Black's e-pawn by playing the usual d4). White's Kingside pawn superiority gives him attacking possibilities on the Kingside in the middlegame and the chance to produce a passed pawn on the e-file in the endgame.

Queen-pawn openings also have distinguishing features. If you regularly play the Queen's Gambit (1. d4 d5 2. c4), sooner or later you will find yourself with an isolated d-pawn. In Diagram 1 the pawn at d4 gives White a spatial advantage, and his control of c5 and e5 make these squares excellent outposts for his pieces, especially Knights. Such an advantage is important in the middlegame, when White can often use his greater mobility to start a direct attack.

The balance of power changes radically in the endgame, when Black has the edge. White's spatial advantage is usually outweighed by his d-pawn's inherent weakness. The d-pawn is weak because (1) it cannot be defended by a pawn, and (2) Black can occupy the square in front of it without fear of being driven away by a pawn attack.

DIAGRAM 1

DIAGRAM 2

Good pieces for Black to put on d5 are his King and Knights, which tend to be the best blockaders. In Diagram 2 for example, Black has maximum pressure against the d-pawn, and White has no better than a draw. In such situations, Black usually tries to blockade and restrain the advance of the d-pawn, while White seeks to push the pawn and exchange it. Although the advance d4-d5 would seem to create a drawish position, White generally gains an advantage, because he is the one who captures on d5 last. The resulting centralization of the capturing piece usually gives White at least a slight initiative, if not a real attack.

The tactics stemming from a timely d4-d5 advance can be quite surprising. Consider Diagram 3's example:

WHITE TO MOVE

DIAGRAM 3

Black has a solid game and is even ahead in development. But White's Queen and Bishop battery are potentially dangerous along the b1-h7 diagonal, though Black's Knight at f6 temporarily holds the fort. Moreover, White's Rook at e1 is well placed, though the e-file is blocked by the pawn at e6. White can realize these potential threats by the immediate advance 1. d5!, because if 1 ... exd5, then 2. Bg5 (threatening 3.Bxf6 and 4. Qxh7 mate) 2 ... g6 (to stop the mate) 3. Rxe7! Qxe7 (3 ... Nxe7 loses to 4. Bxf6) 4. Nxd5 wins material. Vassily Smyslov missed this against Anatoly Karpov in the 1971 Soviet Championship.

Sometimes, White prepares the advance of the d-pawn by moving his Queen off the d-file (say to c2) and deploying his Rook at d1, as in Diagram 4:

WHITE TO MOVE

DIAGRAM 4

White gets the edge by 1. d5! And now after 1 ... exd5 2. Bxd5 Nxd5 (to deal with the threatened discovered attack 3. Bxf7 +, which would win the Bishop at d7) 3. Rxd5, the Bishop falls.

A similar idea was seen in the game Botvinnik-Petrosian from their 1963 match: **1. d4 d5 2. c4 dxc4 3. Nf3 Nf6 4. e3 e6 5. Bxc4 c5 6. 0-0 a6** (to provoke 7. a4, producing a hole at b4 that a Black Knight can use to transfer to d5 for a blockade) **7. a4 Nc6 8. Qe2 cxd4 9. Rd1 Be7 10. exd4 0-0 11. Nc3 Nb4 12. Bg5 Bd7.** (Diagram 5).

DIAGRAM 5

Even with both Black Knights focused on d5, White can advance his d-pawn: **13. d5! Nbxd5 14. Nxd5 exd5 15. Bxd5 Nxd5 16. Rxd5 Bxg5 17. Nxg5 h6 18. Qd3 hxg5 19. Rxd7,** and Black surrendered a pawn (**19 ... Qf6 20. Rxb7**) to reduce the pressure.

These examples show the plan of advancing an isolated d-pawn to d5—an idea usually seen in the Queen's Gambit Accepted. Other systems have their own corresponding plans. In your games and studies, try to associate types of pawn structures with specific openings. Then learn how to play with and against those formations. This will expand your knowledge of opening theory and strengthen your overall play.

CREATING A PASSED PAWN

To Crown a New Queen, Behead Some Foot Soldiers

Basically, endgame theory revolves around the conversion of an extra pawn into a win. A key step in the process is to create a passed pawn. Win a pawn, clear its path, advance it: an easy plan to state but a hard one to execute. Most students sense the significance of passed pawns; yet few appreciate the mechanics of their creation. The following situations illustrate some aspects of creating passed pawns.

Definition of a Passed Pawn

A pawn is passed if it is free to advance toward promotion unhindered by enemy pawns (no enemy pawns block it or guard squares it must pass over):

In the examples above, A shows two passed pawns, B no passed pawns, and C one passed pawn.

Breakthrough Combinations

The next three examples demonstrate the creation of passed pawns in equal and balanced positions. With the enemy King absent, a breakthrough involving a sacrifice materializes after the attacking pawns have reached the fifth rank (especially the candidate passed pawn):

DIAGRAM 1

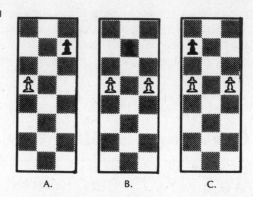

A.   B.   C.

1. W: Kh1, Pa5, b5, c5; B: Kh3, Pa7, b7, c7 (Cozio 1766).

White to move wins with 1. b6, for if 1 ... axb6 then 2. c6 creates a passed a-pawn, and if 1 ... cxb6 then 2. a6 creates a passed c-pawn. Black plays and draws with 1 ... b6 (even though he wins a pawn). Move all pawns back a rank and the combination fails (Black queens and wins!). A similar breakthrough occurs in the next example:

2. W: Ka1, Pe5, f4, g4, h5; B: Ka3, Pe6, f7, g7, h6.

Since this can arise from a line in the Caro-Kann (1. e4 c6 2. d4 d5 3. e5), it is called the Caro-Kann ending. One can steer toward the ending right in the opening.

White to play wins by advancing either pawn. For example: 1. g5 Kb4 2. f5! Kc5 (on 2 ... exf5 White creates a passed King pawn with 3. g6; and on 2 ... hxg5 White gets a passed Rook pawn with 3. f6) 3. f6 and smashes through. The combination works because the defending King is not involved. Sometimes it can be closer and just as helpless, as in the next example:

3. W: Kg4, Pa3, b2, c2, d3, e4; B: Kf6, Pe5, d4, c5, b5, a5.

Black wins by creating a Caro-Kann-like ending with 1 ... a4! A sample variation goes 2. Kf3 (2. Kh5 loses to 2 ... c4) Kg5 3. Ke2 c4! 4. Kd2 Kf4 5. Ke2 c3! 6. bxc3 dxc3 7. Kd1 b4 (a typical breakthrough sacrifice) 8. Kc1 (8. axb4 loses to 8 ... a3 9. Kcl a2) 8 ... b3! 9. cxb3 axb3 10. a4 Ke3 11. a5 Kxd3 12. a6 c2 13. a7 Kc3 and mates next.

Definition of an Outside Passed Pawn

An outside passed pawn is one away from the main theater of action (sometimes also called a distant passed pawn). It is often used to decoy the enemy King (as in the example below, in No. 5, and in No. 6):

4. W: Kg1, Ph2, c2; B: Kg8, Ph7. White wins.

White makes headway with the King and then diverts Black to the Queenside by advancing his expendable decoy: 1. Kg2 Kg7 2. Kg3 Kg6 3. Kg4 Kf6 4. Kh5 Kg7 5. Kg5 h6 + 6. Kh5 Kh7 7. c4 (now is a good time) Kg7 8. c5 Kf7 9. Kxh6 winning. Though other variations achieve the same result, this one is clean-cut and practical. Impulsive students may let victory escape by a premature advance. For example: 1. c4 Kf7 2. c5? Ke6 3. Kg2 Kd5 4. Kg3 Kxc5 5. Kg4 Kd5 6. Kg5 Ke5 7. h4 h5 8. Kxh5 Kf5, and White, unable to extricate his King, has thrown away the win. Unless you are sure that a quick advance works, activate the King first. Before exploring this idea further, we must consider two other concepts.

Pawn Majority

You have a pawn majority when, over any group of consecutive files, your own pawns outnumber the enemy's. Mostly we think in terms of Kingside and Queenside majorities (files *a* through *d* constituting the Queenside, *e* through *h* the Kingside). Majorities, however, can occur over smaller ranges than that. Central majorities are quite common. Healthy majorities are important because they produce passed pawns. When both players have castled on the same side, a majority on the opposite side can be decisive. Thus, the expression "Queenside majority" frequently connotes a tangible advantage.

Capablanca's Rule

In mobilizing pawn majorities, start by advancing the unopposed pawn (the candidate passed pawn, the only one likely to become passed). Take this position: W: Pa2, b2 B: Pa7. 1. a4? is a mistake because Black can immobilize both White pawns with 1 ... a5. Correct is to advance the unopposed pawn (first 1. b4 and then

2. a4). Now we can move to a more complicated version of the example in No. 4:

5. W: Kg1, Pa2, b2, f2, g2, h2; B: Kf8, Pa7, f7, g7, h7 (analysis by Averbakh).

White has a Queenside majority and a potentially passed b-pawn. He should activate the King, create a decoy, and win on the Kingside. For example: 1. Kf1 Ke7 2. Ke2 Kd6 3. b4 Kd5 4. Kd3 f5 (in general, the defender should avoid pawn advances, for they may allow the attacking King to invade on the weakened squares) 5. f4 g6 6. g3 a6 7. a4 Kc6 8. Kd4 Kd6 9. b5 axb5 10. axb5 Kc7 11. Ke5 winning the Kingside pawns. Again it is useful to introduce some general ideas.

Majorities and Their Candidates

- The more distant a passed pawn the better.
- Trade majorities down until the candidate is as distant as possible.

The following chart assigns values to passed pawns and their respective majorities:

EFFECTIVENESS CHART

RATING	KIND OF MAJORITY	DECOY
Best	RP vs. nothing	RP
2nd	RP + NP vs. RP	NP
3rd	RP + NP + BP vs. RP + NP	BP
Worst	RP + NP + BP + CP vs. RP + NP + BP	CP

6. Fischer-Larsen, Candidates Match 1971 (Diagram 2):

With precise play Fischer finds the quickest road to victory: **1. Kd3 Rc5 2. Rxa5** (there go the Rooks) **Rxa5 3. Bxa5 Bxb2 4.a4** (passed pawns must be pushed) **Kf8 5. Bc3!** (there go the Bishops) **5 ... Bxc3** (avoiding the trade soon costs Black his Bishop) **6. Kxc3 Ke7 7. Kd4 Kd6 8. a5 f6 9. a6 Kc6 10. a7 Kb7 11. Kd5 h4** (hoping for 12. gxh4 Kxa7 13. Ke6 f5 14. Ke5 Kb7 15. h5 gxh5 16. Kxf5 Kc7 17. Kg5 Kd7 18. Kxh5 Ke7 19. Kg6 Kf8 with a draw) **12. Ke6 and Black resigned.** It might have ended 12. ... f5 13. Kf6 hxg3 14. hxg3 Kxa7 15. Kxg6 Kb7 16. Kxf5. Fischer's plan was crystal clear: exchange pieces, lure the King away, and invade on the Kingside.

WHITE TO MOVE

WHITE TO MOVE

DIAGRAM 2

DIAGRAM 3

What happens when both Kings are centralized and the majorities offset each other? Not surprisingly, the result may hinge on a single tempo, as in this example from Weinstein-Rohde, Lone Pine 1977, Black to move:

7. W: Kc4, Pa4, b4, f2, g2, g3; B: Kd6, Pb6, e4, f5, g5, h5.

Here the Kingside majority gets there first: 1 ... f4!! (exclamation marks by Jude Acers) 2. gxf4 gxf4 3. Kd4 e3! 4. fxe3 f3 5. gxf3 h4 and wins. In the actual game Black played 1 ... h4? and lost after 2. gxh4 gxh4 3. Kd4 Ke6 4. a5 (decoying) bxa5 5. bxa5 Kd6 6. a6 Kc6 7. Ke5 Kb6 8. Kxf5 Kxa6 9. Kxe4.

8. In the next position, majorities are not as neatly delineated: Fischer-Rubinetti. Buenos Aires 1970 (Diagram 3):

Black has a menacing outside passed pawn. Fischer has a central majority, temporarily immobilized by Black's King pawn (one pawn holding back four). Fischer marshaled his forces with an incisive breakthrough sacrifice: 1 f4! (creating a powerful passed pawn) exf4 2. d4 Kd8 (to protect the Bishop when it retreats) 3. Na5 c5 4. Nc6+ Ke8 5. e5 Bf8 6. Rxc7 and Black rightly resigned in view of 6 ... cxd4 7. e6 with mate sure to follow. How quickly Black succumbed after the breakthrough!

Creating Majorities in the Opening

As stated earlier, favorable majorities can arise directly from opening play. The Exchange Variation of the Ruy Lopez is a good example. After 1. e4 e5 2. Nf3 Nc6 3. Bb5 a6 4. Bxc6 dxc6 5. d4 exd4 6. Qxd4 Qxd4 7. Nxd4 White's Kingside majority is healthy, whereas

Black's Queenside majority is nullified by the double c-pawns. In essence, White is up a pawn. Still, this factor must be viewed in light of the overall position.

In 1940, ex-world champion Euwe tried to demonstrate White's winning chances in the pure King-and-pawn ending:

9. W: Ke1, Pa2, b2, c2, e4, f2, g2, h2; B: Ke8, Pa6, b7, c7, c6, f7, g7, h7.

A sample variation runs 1. Ke2 Ke7 2. Ke3 Ke6 3. f4 c5 4. c4! c6 5. a4 b5 6. b3! f6 7. a5 b4 8. g4 g5 (Averbakh suggests playing for a blockade with g6 instead) 9. e5! gxf4+ 10. Kxf4 fxe5+ 11. Ke4 h6 12. h4 Kf6 13. g5+ hxg5 14. hxg5+ Kxg5 15. Kxe5 and wins on the Queenside, though care is needed.

10. A similar imbalance can occur from a variation of the Caro-Kann. The position arises from 1. e4 c6 2. d4 d5 3. Nc3 dxe4 4. Nxe4 Nf6 5. Nxf6+ exf6. It looks like a mirror image of the Exchange Lopez. The chief difference is that White's "extra" pawn is now on the Queenside.

11. Let's look at a position reflecting the same opening at a later stage: Fischer-Addison, U.S. Open 1957:

DIAGRAM 4

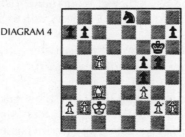

WHITE TO MOVE

Remove the minor pieces and White wins easily—by decoying on the Queenside and then invading on the Kingside. Fischer's technique speaks for itself: 1. Be5! (corralling the Knight) Kh5 2. Kd3 g4 3. b4 (Why take the f-pawn and release the Knight?) a6 4. a4 gxf3 5. gxf3 Kh4 6. b5 axb5 7. a5! (he makes it look so simple) Kh3 8. c6 and forces a Queen on the a-file—a neat breakthrough combination.

12. Finally, one more Fischer example: Fischer-Sandrin, North Central Open 1957:

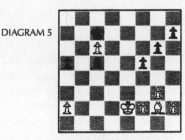

DIAGRAM 5

WHITE TO MOVE

Fischer's extra pawn is countered by the Bishops of opposite colors. These endings are usually drawn because the defender can form unbreakable blockades. Fischer wins by creating a Kingside imbalance, and subsequently, an outside passed pawn (a second front): **1. Bd5 h6** (fearing 2. Bg8) **2. f4!** (preparing to exchange the f-pawn for the g-pawn, thus creating an imbalance on the last two files) **2 ... g5?** (loses immediately; ... Be7 is better) **3. fxg5 hxg5 4. h4** and White's second passed pawn decided the issue.

For many, passed pawns are a subject of total mystery. I have tried to clarify only one small area: how they arise. Necessarily, comment has been brief, analysis sparse. To counteract these limitations, I have carefully selected and arranged examples in graded sequence. Their logic implies what I fail to say. In reviewing this article, scan the page and try to recall some facet of each problem. Find the inner logic; follow its flow.

PAWN POSSES

The Minority Attack

A *minority attack* is an advance by pawns against a greater number of enemy pawns. The objective of this advance is for the side with the fewer pawns to create targets in the enemy pawn structure.

Since minority attacks commonly arise from certain opening systems, such as the Exchange Variation of the Queen's Gambit Declined, textbooks naturally link the concept to the opening phase. Consequently, some amateurs mistakenly think that minority attacks must stem from openings that stress Queenside play. A typical "textbook" pawn structure (Diagram 1) shows that White can assail the Black pawn majority by an eventual b4 and b5.

However, the following two examples should dispel any misconceptions. They show minority attacks occurring not in the opening on the Queenside but in the endgame on the Kingside! Both are fully annotated in Reinfeld's *The Immortal Games of Capablanca*.

Janowski

White to move

Capablanca

DIAGRAM 1   DIAGRAM 2: NEW YORK 1913

A cursory glance shows that material is even and that neither side has a direct threat. Black's doubled pawns, however, are a serious disadvantage. They enable White to obtain a passed e-pawn by means of a minority attack ("minority" because White's two pawns on the g- and h-files attack Black's three pawns on the f-, g-, and h-files). As we shall see, White will need both Rooks to generate threats and thwart enemy activity:

1. g4!

Here is White's idea: he will produce a passed pawn by forcing the exchange of Black's f-pawn. In the carrying out of this plan he will see to it that Black's counterplay is stifled.

1 ... b6

Black plans to advance his doubled pawn, hoping to exchange it for one of White's healthy ones.

2. b4 Kb7 3. Kf2

Inasmuch as Black is unable to prevent g5 (if 3 ... h6 4.h4), White first strengthens his position by centralizing his King. Capablanca was known for careful, methodical preparation; he often achieved decisive positional advantages while his opponents were waiting for him "to do something."

3 ... b5

Threatening 4 ... a5 followed by ... Ra8 with play along the a-file.

4. a4!

Now on 4 ... bxa4 5. Ra5 White gets to the a-file first. It is instructive to watch how Capablanca copes with any sign of counterplay before continuing his Kingside campaign.

4 ... Rd4 5. Rb1 Re5 6. Ke3

Here 6. Rxe5 diverges from White's plan and gives Black a chance to play the freeing c6-c5. Besides, White still needs both Rooks.

6 ... Rd7

Black wisely refrains from 6 ... Rxf5 because after 7. gxf5 Rd7 8.d4 White will control the center, seize the g-file, and soon create a passed pawn.

7. a5!

Closing the Queenside and signaling the start of full-scale Kingside operations.

7 ... Re6 8. Rbf1 Rde7 9. g5 fxg5 10. Rxg5 Rh6 11. Rg3 Rhe6

To stifle the advance of the d-pawn. No better is 11 ... Rh4 (to exert pressure on the h-pawn as well) because of 12. Rf4, with d3-d4 and e4-e5 to follow.

12. h4 g6

Weakening his position.

• General Rule: As defending pawns advance they become easier to attack.

13. Rg5 h6

Obviously trying to deal with the impending h4-h5, but, as already indicated, the pawn advances merely weaken his position.

14. Rg4 Rg7 15. d4 Kc8

Losing time. The King will be forced back to guard the a-pawn.

16. Rf8+ Kb7 17. e5 g5

The next few moves hardly need comment: White's Rooks simply gather in the fruit of his successful minority attack.

18. Ke4 Ree7 19. hxg5 hxg5 20. Rf5 Kc8 21. Rgxg5 Rh7 22. Rh5 Kd7 23. Rxh7 Rxh7

Now that White has achieved a material advantage, he no longer needs to keep both Rooks and is ready to simplify.

24. Rf8 Rh4+ 25. Kd3 Rh3+ 26. Kd2 c5 27. bxc5 Ra3 28. d5, Black resigns—while he still has a chance to do so!

Capablanca

Black to move

Kan

DIAGRAM 3: MOSCOW 1936

Another materially even, two-Rook endgame. This time, however, Capablanca is the one with the doubled pawns. Yet they can't be exploited; they actually give Black dynamic possibilities—use of the a-file, control of the center—and are compact (which makes them easier to defend). Still, to convert these advantages into a win, Black must create more weaknesses in the White camp. It's time for the minority attack.

1 ... g5! 2. h3 h5 3.Rh1
To discourage g5-g4.
3 ... Rd4+ 4. Ke2 Rg8 5. Rd3 Ra5
Black should keep both Rooks until he has a tangible advantage.

• General Rule: The attacker should avoid exchanges until his advantage is concrete.

6. Rhd1 g4 7. hxg4 hxg4 8. Ke3
Fortifying the e-pawn and clearing the second rank for defensive purposes.
8 ... Rh8!
Fearlessly allowing 9. fxg4, for then after 9 ... Rg8 10. Kf3 Rf8+ 11. Ke3 Rf4 only aspirin is left.
9. Rb3 Rh2 10. Rd2 Rd4!

Demonstrating the importance of keeping both Rooks. Black threatens ... Rxd2.

11. Re2 c6

It almost seems that Black's doubled pawns are a positional advantage.

12. Rc3 g3

Threatening ... Rh1-f1 with a strangling bind.

13. Rd3?

Reinfeld points out that after 13. f4 Rh4 14. fxe5 Rdxe4+ 15. Kf3 Rhf4+ 16. Kxg3 Rg4+ 17. Kf3 Rxe2 18. Kxe2 Rxg2+ 19. Kf3 Rh2 20. Kg3! White can probably draw.

13 ... Rh1! 14. f4 Rf1! 15. f5 + Kf6 16. c3 Rxd3 + 17 . Kxd3 d5!

Thank heaven for doubled pawns!

18. b3

As already mentioned, the defender should avoid careless pawn moves: now the a- and c-pawns are critically weakened.

18 ... c4+ 19. bxc4 bxc4+ 20. Ke3 Ra1! 21. Kf3 Rxa3 22. Kxg3 Rxc3 + 23. Kh4

Hoping to sneak in g4 and g5+.

23 ... Rc1! 24. g4 Rh1 + 25. Kg3 d4 26. Ra2 d3 27. Kg2 Re1 28. Kf2 Rxe4 29. Kf3, White resigns. Either 29 ... Rf4+ or 29 ... Rd4 wins quickly.

The minority attack can occur in any phase of the game and in any sector of the board. It is used to inflict weaknesses, open files, and create passed pawns. The attacker—the side with the fewer pawns in that sector—usually needs several pieces, especially a Rook, to support the advance, and he should resist trades until his advantage is tangible. Generally, the defender should avoid pawn moves in the weakened area and counterattack elsewhere.

UNSILENT MAJORITIES

Even Though Material Is Equal, Often You Can Win by Using That Extra Pawn You Have on the Queenside

When you have more pawns on the Queen's wing than your opponent, you have a *Queenside majority.*Healthy majorities have value
because they can produce passed pawns. When both players castle
on the same wing, the threat to create a passed pawn on the
opposite flank can be quite serious. Such a pawn could tie down
the enemy King or divert it at some timely moment.

Futhermore, the sheer distance involved might make it impossible for the King to participate at all, which could then place a great
burden on the other defending pieces. A classic exploitation of this
type of situation comes from the game Marshall-Capablanca (New
York 1909):

BLACK TO MOVE

Black has a potential menace in his Queenside majority, and
should consider a general advance—say a5, followed by b5-b4.
Moreover, his pieces are strongly placed, with his Rook commanding the only open file and his Bishop supporting the lead pawn at
c4. He could try 1 ... Bh3, threatening mate, but that could be dealt
with by 2. Rc1; and if 2 ... Rd2, attacking the b-pawn, then 3. Rb1
defends it. Although White's Rook would then be forced to assume

a passive role, there doesn't seem to be an immediate way to capitalize on its inactivity.

Instead of 1 ... Bh3, White could try a sudden invasion of the seventh rank. After 1 ... Rd2, however, White guards his b-pawn and offers to swap his badly placed Rook with 2. Rc2.

That brings us back to the idea of a broad mobilization of the Queenside starting with 1 ... a5. The problem with advancing right away is that White would then have time to maneuver his King to e2. From there it could defend against an incursion of the Rook, dampening most of Black's advantage. Capablanca therefore acts to prevent this.

1 ... Rd1 +

Preventing White from bringing his King to the center.

2. Kg2

Now Black can safely activate his Queenside pawns.

2 ... a5 3. Rc2

Played in anticipation of b4, as well as to secure the second rank.

3 ... b4 4. axb4 axb4 5. Bf3

This retreat gains time by attacking the Rook. It also enables White to reposition his Bishop at e2 in order to threaten the c-pawn.

If instead White tries 5. Kf3, hoping to centralize his King, his game would probably reach an impasse after 5 ... b3 6. Re2 Rc1. Unless White thereafter finds some hidden resource, Black would follow through by first playing ... Bf5, to secure c2, and in trading Bishops he would then neutralize the opposing Rook by ... Rc2, and eventually make the appropriate breakthrough, c4-c3, sacrificing one pawn to clear a path for the other.

5 ... Rb1

Tying down the White Rook to the second rank.

6. Be2 b3! 7. Rd2

Worse would be 7. Rc3, because 7 ... Rxb2 8. Bxc4 Rc2! wins for Black.

7 ... Rc1

Guarding the c-pawn while preparing to occupy c2.

8. Bd1

To prevent ... Rc2.

8 ... c3

This works because White's Rook is overloaded; it has to guard the Bishop as well as the square b2.

9. bxc3 b2

Marshall must take this pawn and give up his Bishop.
10. Rxb2 Rxd1

The first phase is over. Capablanca exploited his Queenside majority by creating a dangerous passed pawn that forced Marshall to surrender his Bishop. Although the position is now clearly won, it still needs to be handled with great precision. The final stage of the game is an incisive example in the art of using an extra piece.

11. Rc2

White wants to advance his pawn so that he can clear c3 for his Rook. He could then defend the pawn without fear of being driven away by the Bishop. There's also a slight chance that the advancing pawn can become a counterthreat.

11 ... Bf5

Squelching any glimmer of counterplay.

12. Rb2

No better is 12. Ra2.

12 ... Rc1

Capablanca places his Rook behind the passed pawn to restrain its advance. At the same time he maintains the possibility of attacking along White's first and second ranks. Especially notice how the Bishop guards c8, preventing White from establishing his Rook in front of the pawn (after first checking on the back rank).

13. Rb3 Be4 +

Forcing the King to the edge of the board because 14. f3 loses a pawn to 14 ... Rc2 + and 15 ... Bxf3.

14. Kh3 Rc2

Forcing White to push his f-pawn, which opens the seventh rank for Black's Rook.

15. f4 h5

Guarding g4 so that Black threatens a Bishop check at f5, driving the King away from the h-pawn.

16. g4

This still loses a pawn, but at least White gets some breathing space for his King.

16 ... hxg4 + 17. Kxg4

No better is 17. Kg3 because of 17 ... Rg2 + .

17 ... Rxh2 18. Rb4

Possibly hoping to provoke 18 ... f5 + , which might make it easier for White to harass the Black King with his Rook.

18 ... f5 + 19. Kg3

Here, White had to be careful not to compromise his position any further. If he had carelessly played 19. Kg5, then 19 ... Kg7 would have set up a mating net.

Notice how in this variation the extra Bishop stands sentinel, preventing a Rook check at b7. The strength of this centralized piece is the key factor in White's rapid collapse.

19 ... Rc2

There goes another pawn, thanks to the harmonious cooperation of Black's pieces.

20. Rc4 Rxe3 + 21. Kh4

Of course 21. Kf2 merely delays the end.

21 ... Kg7 22. Rc7 + Kf6

Once again we see the Bishop stopping a Rook check, this time at c6.

23. Rd7 Bg2

Threatening 24 ... Rh3 mate.

24. Rd6 + Kg7, White resigns.

Mate is unavoidable. If 25. Rd7 + for example, then 25 ... Kh6 would seal White's fate. Meanwhile, Black is threatening 25 ... Rh3 + , followed by 26 ... Rh5 mate.

This game concisely illustrates two ideas: how to play with a Queenside majority, and how to make best use of an extra piece.

Capablanca's impressive success may have been due largely to his great technique, but before he could apply that talent, he first had to understand the nature of his advantage. Students should realize that only after making a general analysis could Capablanca think in terms of precise moves. Only then could he drive home the win.

SPECIAL EQUATIONS

The Problem of the Rook Pawn

When I was younger my teacher would say, "a pawn is a pawn in any country in the world"—especially just after he had gone out of his way to filch one of my Rook pawns. While often forced to acknowledge his point, now and then I'd make him concede that "some pawns are more equal than others." Rook pawns are flagrant examples. What beginner hasn't felt amazement at his inability to extract the full worth from an extra Rook pawn? Since so many endings hinge on the quality of one's material, it is useful to explore the nature of the Rook pawn's weakness.

In the opening it is easy to understand why Rook pawns are inferior to other kinds: they exert far less influence on the center. While there are times when a Rook pawn can be used to attack the enemy center (such as 5 ... a6 in the Najdorf Sicilian), the central pawn's general superiority is never in doubt. In the ending even more than in the opening, the Rook pawn's essential inadequacy is manifest, although in the ending too, it can have positive features; e.g., when it is outside and passed or contends with a Knight. Usually, its inherent deficiencies far outweigh its dynamic capabilities. Let's begin our investigation by examining the most basic case, in examples 1 and 2:

1. W: Kg6, Ph6; B: Kh8. Drawn.

The problem is that the normal winning move, pawn to the seventh, stalemates. The Rook pawn is a pitiable failure because it does not afford the working room required for basic wins (move everything one file to White's left, and White wins with the move). Often it gives rise to the most bizarre stalemates and positional draws. One can only marvel at their multiplicity. Here is a borderline example:

2. W: Kb6, Pa4; B: Kd7.

White plays and wins with 1. Kb7; Black plays and draws by 1 ... Kc8. In this example, most students seem to think that a draw can be achieved only after occupying b8, but actually c8 is sufficient. For example, after 1 ... Kc8 play might proceed 2. Ka7 Kc7 3. a5 Kc8 4. a6 Kc7 5. Ka8 Kc8 6. a7 Kc7 stalemate.

Sometimes even an extra minor piece is not enough to force a win:

3. W: Kb6, Bd2, Pa6; B: Ka8. Drawn.

The Bishop's inability to influence the crucial corner square renders it useless. Replace the dark-square Bishop with a light-square one or with a Knight and the win is simple. If you really want to flip out, create the following illegal phantasma of a position:

4. Phantasma.

Though ludicrously impossible, it stresses the character of the Bishop's built-in weakness while creating an illusion of mind over matter. Sometimes one can win with the "wrong Bishop," but only if the defending King can be kept from reaching the critical corner, as in No. 5's famous problem by the Russian composer, Troitzky:

5. W: Ke3, Bh3, Ph5; B: Ke8.

1. Be6! Ke7 2. h6 Kf6 2. Bf5! Kf7 4. Bh7! (creating an impenetrable barrier) 4 ... Kf6 (threatening Kg5) 5. Kf4 Kf7 6. Kf5 Kf8 7. Kf6 Ke8 8. Kg7 and wins.

Remarkably, a Knight can prove just as ineffective as a wrong-color Bishop!

6. W: Kg3, Ng5, Ph7; B: Kg7. Drawn.

White's only winning idea consists in first defending the pawn with the King (to free his Knight), but that only leads to stalemate. Therefore, it is impossible to win. The same consequences stem from No. 7!

7. W: Kg3, Nf6, Ph7; B: Kg7. Drawn.

As in the previous example, Black plays back and forth, from g7 to h8 to g7, until White stalemates. In examples 6 and 7, just move everything one rank closer to the White side of the board—or one file to White's left—and the wins are elementary.

Not surprisingly, even having the "right Bishop" can prove fruitless at times, as in No. 8:

8. W: Kf6, Be5, Ph6; B: Kg8, Ph7. Drawn.

White's only hope is based on Black's stumbling into the corner and allowing a discovered mate. Forget it—Black can always play his King to f8. This sets the stage for a problem first shown to me by Julio Kaplan (I do not know its originator):

9. Problem:

Black to play draws by grabbing the pawn and then heading for g8 (establishing a positional draw, as in No. 8). However, White to play can win, not by promoting to a Queen or Rook (giving stalemate), not by making a Knight (which draws after 1 ... Kb7 2. Nd7 Kc8 3. Nf6 Kxd8 4. Nxh7 Ke7 5. Ng5 Kf6 6. h7 Kg7, with a positional draw as in No. 6), but by making another dark-square Bishop!!! After b8 = B!!!, White will eventually be able to force the win of Black's a-pawn and will ultimately reach this position:

10. W: Kf6, Be5 & a7, Ph6; B: Kg8, Ph7.

White to play wins with 1. Bc5—forcing a discovered mate. Here is a legitimate case in which, technically, two Bishops of the same color are needed!

By now you've probably surmised that the Knight wouldn't do much better in No. 11:

11. W: Kf6, Ne5, Ph6; B: Kg8, Ph7. Drawn.

Once the Black King reaches g8 White may as well extend his hand and go home. Notice, we can't blame it all on having the "wrong Knight." Rather, White has the "wrong pawn." For example, shift everything one file to White's left, and White has an elegant win:

12. W: Ke6, Nd5, Pg6; B: Kf8, Pg7.
White to play wins with 1. Kd7 Kg8 2. Ke7 Kh8 3. Nf6! gxf6 4. Kf7, and that's it folks.

One day I was giving an exhibition at a high school when the following position arose:
13. W: Ke6, Nb3, Pa4 & h6; B: Kd8, Nc6, Ph7.
Without much thought I shoved my pawn to a5, and without much thought my opponent immediately removed it. While quietly saying "Will blunders never cease," I suddenly realized that I may have been swindled into a positional draw! Why hadn't I played 1. Kf7, winning easily? Because of my opponent's mile-wide grin it took me a while before I noticed an exquisite conclusion to the whole affair. Play continued 2. Nxa5 Ke8 3. Nc6 Kf8 4. Ne7 Ke8 5. Ng6!! (the only winning idea), and Black resigned. The point is that on 5 ... hxg6 6. h7 queens, and on 5 ... Kd8 White wins with 6. Kf7.

Here is another example which depicts just how lame a Rook pawn can be:
14. W: Kb8, Na5, Pa7; B: Kd8, Bd5.
White would win easily if everything were moved to the right by just one little file (regardless of who moves). However, with a Rook pawn, White wins only if he has the move by 1. Nb7 +, blocking the diagonal leading to the promotion square. With Black to move, the surprising 1 ... Ba8!! holds the fort.

Play might continue 2. Kxa8 (Nb7 + transposes) 2 ... Kc7!! (to draw, Black's King must move to the same-color square as the one occupied by the White Knight). Now, no matter what White does, Black draws by moving his King back and forth from c7 to c8 to c7, etc., and White is unable to extricate the King from the corner. If Black erroneously plays 2 ... Kc8?? (the wrong color) White wins with 3. Nc6 Kc7 4. Ne7, and Black must release the White King from its prison.

The problem illustrates both the weakness of the Rook pawn (no working room on the other side of it) and an intrinsic limitation of the Knight (it can't lose a move in itself; it always does things in twos—from white to black to white).

A similar idea is reflected by the next problem:
15. W: Ka7 Pa6; B: Kc7, Na4.
Replace the Rook pawn with any other pawn and the position is drawn. Having a Rook pawn can be like playing without a full deck. Black to play can win because his Knight can move to the same-color square as that occupied by the White King (and also because the Knight is close enough). Play might proceed 1 ... Nc3 2. Ka8 Nd5! (preventing a7) 3. Ka7 Ne7 4. Ka8 Nc8, forcing White to mate himself. From the original position, if White goes first, or if Black goes first and his Knight is on a dark square (such as a5), then the position is drawn. For example:
16. W: Ka7, Pa6; B: Kc7, Na5.
As in example No. 14, the Knight's inability to lose a move tells: 1 ... Nc4 2. Ka8 Nb6 + 3. Ka7 Nc8 + 4. Ka8 and no progress can be made.

Here is an incredible position I once had in a blindfold exhibition against four opponents:
17. White to play:

I had just won the race to Queen. Curiously, without Black's h-pawn on the board, the game is drawn. For example, **1. Qb4 + Kc2 2. Qa3 Kb1 3. Qb3 + Ka1,** and now White doesn't have time to inch his King closer because of the stalemate. Thus, Queen (with King sufficiently removed) vs. King and RP on the seventh is drawn—one of the few positive features of a Rook pawn in the ending. However, because of the extra (h) pawn, this normally drawn position backfires, and once again the Rook pawn rears its ugly head. After the first three moves already given, I forced mate with **4. Qc2!**

In this endgame survey I have presented examples showing some ways a Rook pawn can be inferior to other kinds. I chose this singular group because I felt it was both useful and instructive. Special emphasis has been placed on endings with an extra minor piece because they *a)* have great practical value and *b)* are not well known. Much more could have been said but not within the allotted space.

There is, however, one more point that should be mentioned. While a stockpile of principles, rules, and basic positions can be useful in any chessplayer's arsenal, one should never forget that *there is no substitute for analysis*. Principles may significantly contribute to an analysis, but they can never replace it. If anything stamps a chess master, it is the ruthless disinterestedness with which he pursues the analytic process. Remember: a general idea is not the end but a means to the end. The end.

5

MINOR PIECES

KNIGHT MOVES

Consider, When Moving Your Knight to the Rim, That Its Chances There Are Quite Often Dim

The old saying "a Knight on the rim is grim" means that Knights are less effective on the outside rows than in the center. The relationship between mobility and location is clear from Diagram 1; the numbers indicate how many squares a Knight can attack from each point:

2	3	4	4	4	4	3	2
3	4	6	6	6	6	4	3
4	6	8	8	8	8	6	4
4	6	8	8	8	8	6	4
4	6	8	8	8	8	6	4
4	6	8	8	8	8	6	4
3	4	6	6	6	6	4	3
2	3	4	4	4	4	3	2

DIAGRAM 1

The closer a Knight is to the center, the greater its mobility (it can attack more squares). Its greatest scope lies within the area bounded by c3-c6-f6-f3-c3. On each of these 16 squares, a Knight attacks eight squares, which is the best it can do in any position. Contrast mobility in the central region with that in the outside rows, and you will see how the Knight's scope is severely hampered near the edge, or the "rim."

A Knight is weakest on the side of the board, and also most vulnerable to enemy surprises. Its restricted mobility and short-range move subjects it to traps. The worst squares for the Knight are the four corners, where it has only two possible moves. Diagram 2A-2D pictures some typical snares:

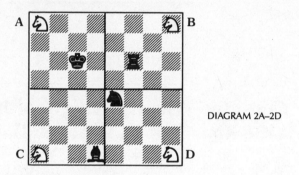

DIAGRAM 2A–2D

In section *A*, the Knight is cornered by the opposing King and may be won if Black successfully plays … Kb7. If Black had a Queen at c6, instead of a King, the Knight would be threatened with immediate capture.

While every piece can trap a cornered Knight, only a King or Queen can capture it singlehandedly. Rooks, Bishops, and Knights (see *B*, *C*, and *D*) need help from a piece or pawn to give a winning attack.

In *B*, the Rook does as well at g7, though it still can't win the Knight by itself. In *D*, we see the glaring difference between a centralized Knight and a cornered one. In *C*, we have a version of the most typical trap of all, where the Bishop is said to "corral" the Knight. Replace the Bishop with a Queen, and the Knight is under immediate fire.

In *C* and *D*, the Knight's precarious situation can be exploited by a pawn attack (from b2 and g2 respectively). The assailing pawn threatens to become a Queen either by advancing or by capturing the Knight. The Knight cannot defend against this type of threat unless it can move with a gain of time (for example, if it can check and reposition itself).

Diagram 3A-3C shows that a Knight on the edge fares little better than one in the corner:

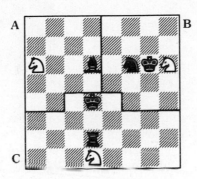

DIAGRAM 3A–3C

The famous bishop corral is shown again in section A. A more typical example occurs when a White Knight at c3 moves to a4 to attack a Black Bishop at c5; the Bishop slides over to d4, trapping the Knight. A Knight so trapped can be attacked by a pawn from b5.

Diagram 4 shows a decisive Bishop corral from the game Fischer-Addison (U.S. Open 1957). After the immobilizing 1. Be5!, Fischer was able to force through a passed pawn: 1 ... Kh5 2. Kd3 g4 3. b4 a6 4. a4 gxf3 5. gxf3 Kh4 6. b5 axb5 7. a5 Kh3 8. c6.

DIAGRAM 4: WHITE TO MOVE

In Diagram 3B, the more centralized Black Knight and aggressive King line up to win the Knight outright. The Diagram 5 position (Dzindzichashvili-Whitehead, U.S. Championship 1983) provides an example from actual play. The game continued **1. Nc4 + Kc6 2. Nxa5 + Kb5,** and White lost his Knight.

DIAGRAM 5: WHITE TO MOVE

DIAGRAM 6: BLACK TO MOVE

There is a geometric beauty in Diagram 3's Sections *B* and *C*. In the latter, the trap also works with the King at d3. Neumann-Steinitz, shown in Diagram 6, illustrates this theme. Steinitz won the Knight after **1 ... Rf1 2. Nb2 Rb1** (the Knight also falls after 2 ... Ra1 and 3 ... Kc3) **3. Na4 Rb4.**

A Knight is equally vulnerable on the second row in from the edge (Diagram 7A–B):

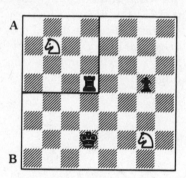

DIAGRAM 7A–7B

In *A*, the Knight is trapped, and any man, except an opposing Knight, can give the winning attack. Another trap: Black King at d5 and Rook at a8. White wins the Knight by Kc6. The point in *B* is that, with the Black King so placed, White's Knight is trapped if both f4 and h4 are guarded. Black wins the Knight (assuming no interference from other White forces) by moving his King to f2. The trap also works with a Bishop at g5, a Knight at g6, or a Rook at g4 (when the Knight is attacked at the same time).

There are times when a Knight can be well posted on the flank, especially if the center is blocked. But usually it's best in the center. So, next time you're considering Na4 think twice. You may find the Knight's future there is slim, or dim, or even grim.

CLERICAL DUTIES

Sometimes Devious, Sometimes Bold, the Bishop Is a Handy Fellow if You Know How to Treat Him Properly

When used properly, a Bishop is a dynamic force. With its long-range muscle and ability to sweep the board in a single move, it can suddenly, decisively shape the game. But since it is confined to diagonal pathways, it has certain limitations that can get it into trouble quickly. Here are a few things to heed:

• *Don't give pointless checks.* This is an easy mistake to make with a Bishop, especially in the opening. A misguided check can lead to a waste of time and sometimes loss of material. After 1. e4 e5 2. Nf3 d6, for example, 3. Bb5 + doesn't make much sense. Black has several adequate responses, not the least of which is 3 ... c6, forcing the Bishop to move again.

• *Don't develop Bishops prematurely.* One reason for the principle "Knights before Bishops" in the opening is that Knight moves tend to be slightly less committal than Bishop moves. Knights simply have fewer options. You can't be as certain about where to put your Bishops. If you develop a Bishop too soon, and have to change your plans; you may have to move it again. If the Bishop could have gone to the second square at once, you've wasted a move. By holding the Bishop back a move or two, you may actually save time. Try in the opening to find the best square for your Bishops, and get them there as soon as realistically possible. But at the same time, play flexibly. Don't commit yourself to a scheme you may shortly have to change.

• *Don't develop a Bishop and block a center pawn.* For example, after 1. e4 e5 2. Nf3 Nc6, the move 3. Bd3 is poor development. This gets a piece out, but wastes time because it blocks the d-pawn, forcing White to move the b-pawn to develop his dark-square Bishop. Being unable to move the d-pawn will hinder White's thematic attempts to open the game and exert pressure against Black's center. Of course, 3. Bd3 also puts the Bishop on a blocked diagonal, but more on that later.

• *Don't make unnecessary pawn moves to develop a Bishop.* This generally happens when both the KP and the KNP are moved in order to develop the KB. Unless there is a specific reason for moving both pawns, advancing either one is sufficient to release the Bishop. Moreover, in moving both pawns, you diminish control over the square KB3, rendering it weak and vulnerable to enemy exploitation.

• *Don't exchange a flanked Bishop (unless necessary).* If you made the effort to fianchetto a Bishop (developing it to a. N2 square), it's time-wasting to suddenly trade it away without good reason. Once it's gone, both the B3 and R3 squares on that flank are weakened and prone to enemy occupation. If your King is castled on that side, your opponent may invade on the vulnerable squares with disastrous consequences. Thus, in Diagram 1 White should play 1. Bh1, preserving his flanked Bishop.

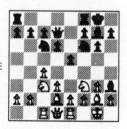

DIAGRAM 1: WHITE TO MOVE

• *Don't block your Bishops with pawns.* When developing a Bishop, try to place it on a clear diagonal. If a Bishop is already developed, avoid fixing pawns on squares that obstruct its range. In Diagram 2, 1. d5 drives away the Knight on c6, but only at the cost of closing the Bishop's a2-g8 diagonal. Even if the pawns are not fixed and can still move, it's best to place them on squares the opposite color of your Bishop (unless they absolutely must be guarded by the Bishop, or visa versa). Doing so reduces the Bishop's scope and leaves the other squares unprotected.

DIAGRAM 2: WHITE TO MOVE

• *Don't trade a developed Bishop for an undeveloped piece.* Usually, the undeveloped piece is a Knight, and the trade loses a lot of time. In Diagram 3, for example, 1. Bxb8 gives up a developed piece, develops the opponent's Rook, and saves Black additional time, for he no longer has to develop the Knight at b8.

DIAGRAM 3: WHITE TO MOVE

• *Don't automatically pin or make pin-like attacks against Knights.* Sometimes a Knight attacked in this way can move forward and counterattack the Bishop. Thus, after 1. d4 d5 2. Nf3 Nf6 3. Bg5, White should be prepared for 3 ... Ne4, when the hunter becomes the hunted. The Knight in Diagram 4 was merely attacked and not pinned. But even in the case of real pins, the Knight may be able to move anyway. For example, after 1. e4 d6 2. d4 g6 2. Nf3 Bg7 4. Bc4, White can answer the ill-conceived pin 4 ... Bg4? with 5. Bxf7 + , for 5 ... Kxf7 6. Ng5 + regains the piece with a winning game.

DIAGRAM 4: WHITE TO MOVE

• *Watch out for pawn traps.* Perhaps the best known is the Noah's Ark Trap in the Ruy Lopez. After 1. e4 e5 2. Nf3 Nc6 3. Bb5 a6 4. Ba4 Nf6 5. 0-0 d6 6. d4 b5 7. Bb3 Nxd4 8. Nxd4 exd4, White shouldn't play 9. Qxd4, when 9 ... c5 attacks the Queen and also threatens 10 ... c4. It's easy to stumble into such a trap.

• *Beware of fork tricks.* This tactic can destroy your center and disrupt your game by taking advantage of a poorly placed Bishop (usually the KB) and an insecure center pawn (usually the KP). In the Diagram 5 position (achieved after 1. e4 e5 2. Nf3 Nc6 3. Nc3 Nf6 4. Bb5 Bc5 5. 0-0 h6?), White can safely play 6. Nxe5. If then 6 ... Nxe5, the fork trick 7. d4 regains the piece and gives White a powerful initiative. In similar situations, the fork trick may be averted by protecting the KP with the QP or withdrawing the Bishop at QB4 to QN3.

DIAGRAM 5: WHITE TO MOVE

Throughout history, at different times and in various countries, the Bishop has been known as a sage, a count, an old man, and a fool. But since the end of the 15th century, when it was given its present move, a Bishop has been able to reach e7 from e1 in eight moves in any of 483 different ways—most of which violate the spirit of sound play. In chess, there are many more ways to go wrong than to go right. Learn the strengths and weaknesses of each piece, and at least you have a fighting chance.

IN PRAISE OF BISHOPS

Deployed Properly, Bishop Pairs Produce Won Endgames

The first person to get a new slant on the advantage of having two Bishops was Wilhelm Steinitz, but his views were too oblique for the time. A century later, many of us know enough to play for two Bishops, but a lot of us still can't play with them.

While no article can rectify a chronic problem, I hope this one at least provides a few insights into why two Bishops are generally superior to either a Bishop and a Knight or two Knights.

In the endgame, certain overlapping arguments favor the Bishop pair. Although most of these points seem minuscule when considered separately, their sum total can be overwhelming.

By working in harmony, the two Bishops usually are more able to:

• *Negate the chief failing of each Individual Bishop.* Though a single Bishop can only guard squares of one color, Bishop pairs can combine to guard all squares.

• *Control the center.* Bishops don't have to be close to the center to influence it.

• *Restrict enemy movement.* This is true because Bishops can often "stalemate" an enemy Knight and can also more easily harass the enemy King than can a Knight.

• *Force weakening pawn moves.* Bishops can readily attack pawns from far away or from behind.

• *Support the invasion of their own King.* Bishops are able to induce weaknesses and gain tempi.

• *Create favorable exchanges.* The Bishops' greater mobility often allows simplification to endings of good Bishop versus bad Bishop or good Bishop versus bad Knight.

• *Contend with advancing pawn masses.* Bishops, even when driven away, can still attack the pawns and the squares they must pass over.

• *Convoy a passed pawn to promotion.* Bishops can guard square after square in the pawn's path. This is so important that an outside passed pawn supported by two Bishops almost always wins in normal circumstances.

How It Works

A good example that shows how to play with a pair of Bishops comes from the game Taubenhaus-Tarrasch (Monte Carlo 1903):

BLACK TO MOVE

White has a Kingside pawn majority, and Black has a preponderance on the Queenside. Pawn imbalances ordinarily favor the two Bishops because they are better suited to producing passed pawns while neutralizing enemy pawn advances.

Even though Black's majority in this case is somewhat nullified by the doubled c-pawns, the synergistic cooperation between the two Bishops still gives Black the playing edge. If White doesn't undertake some kind of reasonable action, the Black Bishops might gradually (a) cramp the enemy position, (b) weaken the White pawn structure and then (c) escort the Black King deep into the White camp.

Here, in order to induce weaknesses, Black played the consistent
1 ... Bb1!
White is forced to push his a-pawn and weaken b3. For reasons that should become clear later, this weakening will facilitate the creation of a passed pawn for Black.

2. a3 Bd3 +
Black was in time trouble and had to make moves. Yet, 2 ... Bd3 + also has the merit of driving the White King either from the center or onto squares needed by his pieces—d2 for the Knight and f2 for the Bishop.

3. Ke1 Kd5 4. Bf2
It is difficult to attack targets that can move but, as former World Champion Max Euwe points out, White shouldn't try to fix the h-

pawn first with 4. h3 because, after 4 ... b6 5. Bf2 Ke4, the Black King will plunder away.

4 ... h3 5. g3

Although not the best, this move seems more natural than the ugly (but better) 5. gxh3 which, after 5 ... b6 (in order to free the King from defending the c-pawn) 6. Be3 (to guard the f-pawn) 6 ... Ke4 7. Kf2, would still give White some counterattacking possibilities—8. h4 and 9. Ng5+, for example.

Not surprisingly, if White reacts too sharply with 5. g4? (trying to mobilize his Kingside majority and produce a passed pawn), he loses something after 5 ... Ke4 6. Ng1 Kxf4 7. Bxc5 Kxg4 8. Bxa7 Bg5, and Black threatens both Bc1 and Bf4.

5 ... b6

Now, the Black King is free to meander.

6. Ng1

This move just wastes time. Better is to keep out the Black King with 6. Nd2.

6 ... Bf5

Notice that the Bishops not only give Black better attacking possibilities but also provide him with greater defensive resources.

7. Nf3

Of course, White doesn't want to leave his Knight back on g1, where it could be corralled if Black moves his Bishop to g4—not necessarily now, but at some critical point a few moves ahead

7 ... Ke4 8. Nd2+

It is worse to play 8. Ng5+ because, after 8. ... Bxg5 9. fxg5 Kd3 10. Kd1 Bg4+ 11. Kc1 Ke2, the Black King invades decisively. Observe how the Bishops in this variation enable Black to gain time in order to maneuver in with his King.

8 ... Kd3

The overt and reserve powers of the two Bishops have enabled Black to march his monarch into the White heartland. Barring total blockade or timely tactics, a Bishop pair is almost always able to secure a beachhead for their own King.

9. Nf1

It's not too difficult to see that 9 ... Kc2 blunders a piece to 10. Ne3+, so Black first decides for safety's sake to reposition his light-squared Bishop.

9 ... Be4 10. Ne3 Be7

By overpowering his c-pawn, Black can soon begin the inevitable march of his Queenside foot soldiers.

11. g4

White feels constrained to try something before being driven into the sea, but the Black Bishops will have no trouble coping with this last-ditch thrust.

11 ... b5 12. g5

The White pawns seem adrift in a Bermuda Triangle of Black pieces and may soon be swallowed up. No better was the logical 12. f5, which would have met with the unpleasant 12 ... Bg5.

At least after 12. g5 White can harbor the vague hope of sacrificing his g-pawn to create a passed e-pawn (which wouldn't go any farther anyway).

12 ... a5 13. Kd1

White has to guard c2 in order to free his Knight.

13 ... b5 14. cxb4 cxb4 15. axb4 axb4 16. Nc2

One last trap. If Black now blindly plays 16 ... b3, his eyes will be closed for good after 17. Ne1 mate. But Tarrasch is the kind of player who actually looks at the board before moving.

16 ... c3 17. bxc3

No better was 17. b3 because, after 17 ... Bf3 + 18. Kc1 Bd5 19. Na1 Ke2, the end is in sight.

17 ... b3

Here we see the advantage derived from the early weakening of the White Queenside. Because the White a-pawn had to abandon control of b3, nothing now can stop the Black b-pawn from Queening. If 18. Ne1 + , then 18 ... Kxc3, and the b-pawn sails through:

WHITE RESIGNS

Put It on Paper

Two Bishops usually constitute a true advantage. The reasons for that advantage and the ways to exploit it have been outlined in this article. In chess, there are many other similar generalities, of great practical value, that are not so difficult to learn.

If you'd like to build up your knowledge of these fundamental concepts, you can start by following a definite course of action. Whenever you come upon an idea worth preserving, try to express it in your own words. Then record your thoughts in a looseleaf notebook or on index cards and file them away. To drive home your efforts, read through all your notes on a regular basis.

It may or may not help you to become a master, but it can help you master a plan.

KNIGHTLY PERFORMANCE

In Certain Positions, a Sprightly Knight Can Dance Circles Around a Long-legged Bishop

No principle is absolute. Each one has its limitations, exceptions and modifying provisions. So, though a Bishop is preferable to a Knight in most positions, certain situations actually favor the Knight. The Knight tends to get the upper hand when it can:

- Exploit its ability to guard squares of both colors.
- Occupy unassailable posts in the enemy terrain.
- Capitalize on closed positions that severely hamper the bishop.

Still, a Bishop may have such resilience that often a Knight's superiority must be overwhelming before a game can be won. The following example is a case in point:

WHITE TO MOVE

White has an extra pawn, but it's doubled and on the a-file to boot; it doesn't seem too material. The other obvious difference is that White has a Knight and Black a Bishop. To determine which minor piece is best, we should examine the character of the pawn structure. Since the pawns are blocked and fixed, since they cannot move, it is less risky to make general assessments and therefore to form plans.

Observe that Black's pawns are stuck on squares that obstruct the Bishop but not the Knight. Meanwhile, the Bishop has no specific targets while the Knight can zero in on c6 and a6. The Bishop might just finish the game as a spectator.

Turning to other features, we see that White has a spatial advantage because his pawns are further advanced. Moreover, White's King is on the frontier, poised for invasion, while Black's is merely digging trenches, holding the fort.

The only real drawback for White is that his Knight can't gain or lose a move in itself. The point is that a Knight must guard an entirely different set of squares from move to move, whereas a Bishop can temporize without having to give up control of a key diagonal.

This is where White's doubled pawn comes in. It provides two free moves whenever needed. Without these two tempi, the game would be drawn, regardless of White's positional advantages. *Never underestimate the value of extra material. Even when it doesn't win perforce, it may indirectly influence factors that do.*

White can best exploit his leverage by first tying down the Bishop. This can be done by maneuvering the Knight to b4, attacking both Black weaknesses and imprisoning the Bishop on b7. The real battle then becomes a dance of death between the Kings. By wisely using his additional tempi, White will try to plant his monarch on d6 in order to attack the c-pawn twice. Even if Black can twice defend it (say, King at b7 and Bishop at b5), White can thereafter win the pawn with a Knight check from d8.

That's the plan in words. Here it is in moves:

1. Ng4 + Ke6

Black really has no choice, for taking the Knight reduces to a lost King-and-pawn ending. On 1 ... Bxg4 for example, White's doubled pawn would prove decisive after 2. Kxg4 Kg6 3. Kf4 Kf6 4. a3! Ke6 5. Kg5 Ke7 6. Kf5 Kf7 7. Ke5 Ke7 8. a4! Kd7 9. Kf6 Kd8 10. Ke6 Kc7 11. Ke7 Kc8 12. Kd6 Kb7 13. Kd7. Notice that White needs both tempi to win in this line, which is why the pawn must start at a3 and not a2!

2. Ne5 Bb7

This is forced because 2 ... Bd7 permits a winning simplification by 3. Nxd7.

3. Nd3 Kf6 4. Nb4

This first part of the plan is over. Black must now rely on King moves.

4 ... Ke6 5. Kg5 Ke7

Black's diagonal opposition is meaningless because White has two extra pawn moves that ensure further inroads into the opposing camp.

6. Kf5 Kf7

Also possible is 6 ... Bc8 + 7. Ke5 Bb7. Yet that merely transposes into the game continuation.

7. Ke5 Ke7 8. a3!

White finally spends a tempo in order to sustain his penetrating drive.

8 ... Kd7 9. Kf6 Bc8

Now at least the Bishop can shuttle between b7 and c8 because the c-pawn is also guarded by the Black King. White therefore will have to reposition his Knight before further progress can be made.

10. Nd3 Bb7

Note how Black is unable to initiate any form of counteraction and must sit back and wait for White to try something.

11. Ne5 + Kd8 12. Ke6 Kc7 13. Ke7 Bc8 14. Nd3

White's idea is to deploy his Knight to e6, further driving back the Black King and enabling the White one to reach d6.

14 ... Bh3

Instead of staring at the walls of pawns. Black decides to transfer the Bishop to the b5-a4 diagonal, hoping to get some fresh air.

15. Nf4 Bf1

As already indicated, it would be futile to keep the Bishop on the c8-h3 diagonal in order to exchange it for the Knight because the pawn ending is dead lost.

16. Ne6 + Kb7 17. Kd6

Mission accomplished.

17 ... Bb5

What else?

18. Nd8 +

DIAGRAM 2

And Black threw in the score sheet.

Bishops are usually better than Knights, but chess books often exaggerate this disparity. They tell you that a Knight on the rim is dim—and then prove it.

Try not to consider chess positions so mechanically. Sometimes a retreating Knight is really advancing backward. Sometimes we have to stop and think.

KNIGHT BLINDNESS

Handled Properly, Your Faithful Horse Can Drive Away Danger—Handled Improperly, It Can Drive You Crazy

A knight can be the most frustrating distance between two points. Just try to wend one of these struggling pieces through a hostile maze to catch a runaway pawn. The horse, on the other hand, can break your heart even up close. Nothing is more pathetic than a Knight sitting on its own back rank, helpless, attacked by a pawn about to Queen.

If you've had a few Knightmares in the past, I suggest you check your grip on fundamentals. Offhand, can you tell me how many moves it would take for a Knight starting on f3 to reach e3? or e4? Or f4, f5 and d5?

Let's "Capablancasize" a bit more. Are you sure you know under what conditions a lone Knight can fend off a monstrous passed pawn? For those who have doubts (Descartes, et al.), the following rules of thumb may clear the picture while providing some groundwork for serious study.

(Note: These examples deal with cases where the Knight, unaided by its King, must hold the fort. The side with the Knight obviously draws if it sacrifices a piece for the pawn.)

• Axiom 1: The Knight draws if it can occupy any square in the pawn's path, including the promotion square (with one exception):

DIAGRAM 1: WHITE DRAWS

If Black attacks the Knight by ...

1... Kf2

... then White can maintain a safe grip on e1 by moving the Knight to either c2 or d3. The piece can't be dislodged no matter what. For example:

2. Nd3 + Ke3 3. Ne1 Kd2

The position only repeats on 3 ... Kf2.

4. Ng2

Or even 4. Nf3 +. No progress can be made.

Exception: A RP on the seventh rank:

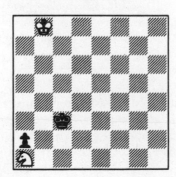

DIAGRAM 2: BLACK WINS

White is unable to avert the loss of his Knight even with the move. The hapless horse is doomed because the corner file offers no room to maneuver. The only possible draw in this kind of situation arises when the defending King can get back in time to create stalemate after the Knight is captured.

DIAGRAM 3:
WHITE TO PLAY
AND DRAW

1. Kd3 Kxa1
What else? Now White saves the game with
2. Kc2, draw.
It's a stalemate.
• Axiom 2: The Knight draws if it can attack the pawn in such a way that, if the pawn moves out of attack, the Knight can win the pawn (or the new Queen) by a forking check:

DIAGRAM 4:
WHITE TO PLAY
AND DRAW

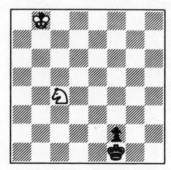

1. Nd2 + Ke2
For an explanation of 1 ... Ke1, see the next position.
2. Ne4!
Forcing Black to promote the pawn.
2 ... f1 = Q 3. Ng3 +

And the Queen is won. But what would happen if Black plays 1 ... Ke1 instead of 1 ... Ke2?

DIAGRAM 5:
WHITE TO PLAY
AND DRAW

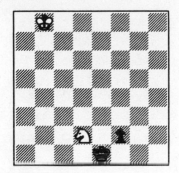

White draws by shifting the Knight to the other side of the pawn. Simply 1. Nf3+, followed by 2. Nh2, will stop Black from making any horseway. Nevertheless, although this maneuver works against Bishop pawns and center pawns, the next example shows it doesn't succeed against pawns on the Knight and the Rook files.

DIAGRAM 6:
WHITE TO MOVE

1. Ne2+ Kf1

Why not 1 ... Kf2?? because 2. Nf4 wins the pawn with a forking check.

2. Ng3+ Ke1

And the pawn squirms through.

• Axiom 3: The Knight draws if it can occupy any square in the RP's path, other than the promotion square:

DIAGRAM 7: A DRAW

Here the Knight can save the day by a forking check. For example:

1 ... Kg2

Or 1 ... Kg3 2. Nf1+ Kg2 3. Ne3+ Kf2 4. Ng4+ Kg3 5. Ne3, transposing into the text.

2. Ng4 Kg3 3. Ne3

And now 3 ... h2 4. Nf1+ snares the pawn.

Note how the Knight is able to stay in contact with h2 by pivoting around a related block of four key points: h2-g4-e3-f1. This might seem quadrivial, but it's important to realize the Knight can observe h2 from e3 because of the possibility of a forking check.

Sometimes the Knight can be so stationed that it hinders the approach of the enemy King, even when its own King can't immediately participate. It does this by establishing a barrier, a virtual no-man's land, that forces the attacking King to take a circuitous, time-wasting path.

In this final example (drawn from Averbakh), the Knight is able to retard the enemy King's advance by threatening to shift to a square on the circuit (g4), with check. This resource gives the defending King ample time to saunter into town:

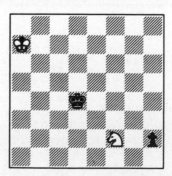

DIAGRAM 8:
BLACK TO MOVE

1 ... Kc3
But not 1 ... Ke3 or 1 ... Ke5 because of 2. Ng4+.
2. Kb6 Kd2 3. Kc5 Ke1 4. Nh1 Kf1 5. Kd4 Kg2 6. Ke3 Kxh1 7. Kf2 draw.
Again, it's stalemate.

The "ABCs of Chess" was conceived with the nascent tournament player in focus. It therefore often deals with elementary questions that seem to give new meaning to the words "tedious and dull." Indeed, few of us want to dwell on things we think we already know.

Let's face it. It takes a very unusual mind to study the basics. In fact, it usually takes a grandmaster.

THE BISHOP-AND-KNIGHT MATE

A Practical Demonstration

Everybody "knows" the basic Bishop-and-Knight mate, but few can actually demonstrate it. Some experts recommend studying the mating process because it is a model of the combined powers of the two pieces, whereas other experts discourage amateurs from studying it because it arises so seldom in actual play.

The Bishop-and-Knight mate should be explored because certain aspects of it carry over to a wide range of practical endings, especially the way the two pieces cooperate to rope off entire sections of the board. Since space is a factor not only in the endgame, knowing how to coordinate these two pieces is useful in other phases of the game as well.

You don't have to devour every detail to learn how to play this ending. You can assimilate the key ideas simply by examining the formations and patterns presented here. To strengthen your grasp of these ideas, work out the sample variations and notes. And if you're still thirsty for variations, turn to the standard texts (Averbakh or Cheron, for example).

A Word of Advice

In some positions you may not be able to mate in fewer than 30 moves, and you may exceed the 50-move drawing rule (if no capture or pawn move occurs in 50 moves, the game is a draw). At first, don't worry about accuracy. Instead, try to develop an overview of the subject. Once you know what has to be done, then you can learn the precise way to do it. Don't make the mistake of trying to know everything before you know something.

How Mate Is Forced

To force checkmate you must drive the lone King to a corner square that is the same color as the squares controlled by your Bishop. With a light-square Bishop, mate can be forced only in the h1 or a8 corner; with a dark-square Bishop, only in the a1 or h8 corner. The term "right corner" is used for a corner in which mate can be forced; "wrong corner" for the other kind.

Two Typical Mating Patterns

In Diagram 1 the Knight could also be on d7 and the Bishop on any square along the g2-b7 diagonal. In Diagram 2 the Knight could also be on a6 or d7.

| DIAGRAM 1 | DIAGRAM 2 | DIAGRAM 3 |

It is easy to mate once the King is trapped in the right corner. The problem is to force it there in the first place. Although this might require precise maneuvering, you can make the job easier by thinking in terms of specific schemes. For example, Diagram 3 shows a simple forcing situation: Black must retreat.

Three Related Nets

Before you can drive the King into the right corner, you must restrict its movement. For this you may find it helpful to remember three interrelated nets and their mirror images. The nets are shown in Diagram 4, their mirror images in notation:

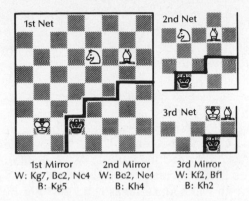

DIAGRAM 4

1st Mirror	2nd Mirror	3rd Mirror
W: Kg7, Bc2, Nc4	W: Bc2, Ne4	W: Kf2, Bf1
B: Kg5	B: Kh4	B: Kh2

These three nets (and their respective mirrors) are related in that each is a stage in the same confining process: in all three the lone King clearly has no escape. The 1st net can usually be created even without your opponent's realizing it. From there you maneuver your King closer, square by square, tightening the 1st net into the 2nd net (or its mirror). Finally, by the same gradual maneuvering, you squeeze the 2nd net into the 3rd (or its mirror). As you try it, you will sometimes find it useful to waste a move by moving the Bishop along the last diagonal it had to control (I'll explain this later).

Three Corresponding Triangles

Notice that in Diagram 5 each net is a right triangle. The 1st net is the triangle b1-h1-h7, the 2nd net d1-h1-h5, and the 3rd net f1-h1-h3. Notice also that the Bishop occupies the hypotenuse (the side

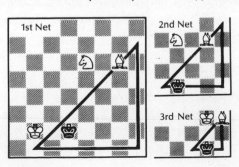

DIAGRAM 5

opposite the right angle) of each triangle in succession: first the b1-h7 diagonal, then the d1-h5 diagonal, and finally the f1-h3 diagonal. Indeed, the crux of the whole restricting process is to transfer the Bishop from the 1st hypotenuse to the 2nd and finally to the 3rd. (The rudiments of this system can be traced back to 1780, but it wasn't published as a system until 1923.) The following analysis demonstrates the whole process, from the 1st net to mate. Try to follow the general course of play without getting lost in particulars. The main line of play is in boldface type, the notes in parentheses.

Starting from the 1st net:

1. Bc2 (to drive the lone King back, if possible to the h1 corner) **1 ... Ke3** (staying close to the center) **2. Kc1** (to be able to play Kd1 preventing Black from reaching e2) **2 ... Ke2 3. Bg6** (a waiting move forcing Black to give ground) **3 ... Ke3 4. Kd1 Kf2** (4 ... Kf3 5. Kd2 Kf2 6. Bh5 and White will soon establish the 2nd net by shifting his Knight to e4 and the Bishop to g4 or e2) **5. Kd2 Kf3 6. Kd3 Kg4** (staying as far as possible from the h1 corner and preventing the Bishop from reaching h5 to shorten the hypotenuse; on 6 ... Kf2 7. Bh5 tightens the net) **7. Ke3 Kh4** (still guarding h5) **8. Kf4 Kh3 9. Bh5** (mission accomplished: the Bishop controls the hypotenuse of the 2nd triangle and has narrowed Black's territory) **9 ... Kg2** (trying to run away; but on 9 ... Kh4 10. Be2 Kh3 11. Kg5 + or Nc5 and 12. Ne4 establishing the mirror image of the 2nd net) **10. Nc5** (or Ng5) **Kf2 11. Ne4 + Kg2** (on other King moves White replies the same way) **12 Bg4** (arriving at the 2nd net; now White moves his King in, squeezing Black into the 3rd net) **12 ... Kf1 13. Kf3** (or Ke3) **Ke1 14. Ke3 Kf1 15. Kd2 Kg2 16. Ke2 Kg1** (if 16 ... Kh2 17. Kf2 Kh1 18. Bh3 Kh2 19. Ng5 Kh1 20. Bg2 + Kh2 21. Nf3 mate) **17. Bh3** (seizing the hypotenuse of the final triangle) **17 ... Kh2 18. Bf1 Kg1 19. Ng5** (preparing to guard h2) **19 ... Kh1** (on 19 ... Kh2 20. Kf2 Kh1 21. Bg2 + Kh2 22. Nf3 mate) **20. Kf2** (obviously not 20. Nf3 stalemate) **20 ... Kh2 21. Nf3 + Kh1 22. Bg2 mate.** These variations clearly depict how the three pieces work harmoniously.

Starting from the Wrong Corner

The nets are foolproof, but sometimes the lone King avoids the nets and retreats to a wrong corner. We therefore need a method of driving the King from a wrong corner to a right one:

DIAGRAM 6

This is done by gradually controlling square after square along the outer row. Here White can systematically drive Black to either a8 or h1. White's King is ideally placed on f6, equidistant from both light-square corners. By rotating the board, you can see that if the wrong corner were a8, White's King should start on c6; if it were a1, the King should start on c3; and if it were h1, the King should start on f3.

The first square White must control is h8, either by Nf7 or Ng6. To drive Black's King to h1, White should play Ng6; to drive it to a8, White should play Nf7. Let's look first at driving the King to a8:

1. Nf7+ Kh7 (on 1 ... Kg8 White still plays 2. Be4) **2. Be4+ Kg8** (since White wants to play Bh7 to guard g8, the next square along the outer row, he must waste a move) **3. Bf5** (as I indicated above, you can waste a move in this ending by moving the Bishop along the last diagonal it had to control: in this case, the b1-h7 diagonal) **3 ... Kf8 4. Bh7** (next White must maneuver his Knight to guard f8) **4 ... Ke8 5. Ne5** (preventing escape via d7 and repositioning the Knight to guard f8 from d7).

Black can now move closer to the wrong corner by Kf8 or make a run for it by Kd8. Sample variations for each possibility follow:

A: Passive Defense

5 ... Kf8 6. Nd7+ Ke8 7. Ke6 Kd8 8. Kd6 Ke8 (on 8 ... Kc8 9. Nc5, and if 9 ... Kd8 10. Bg6 Kc8 11. Bh5 [or f7] Kd8 12. Nb7 + continues the confining process; if 9 ... Kb8 10. Kc6 Kc8 11. Nb7; if 10 ... Ka7 11. Kc7 and the Black King is trapped) **9. Bg6+** (White eats up another square along the back row) **9 ... Kd8 10. Nc5** (preparing to guard d8 from b7, but not from e6 which would interfere with the Bishop) **10 ... Kc8** (since White wants to play Nb7, he needs to waste a move with his Bishop) **11. Bf7** (or Bh5) **Kd8** (or 11 ... Kb8 12. Kc6 and the

Black King will be trapped as in an earlier variation) **12. Nb7+ Kc8 13. Kc6 Kb8 14. Kb6 Kc8** (or 14 ... Ka8 15. Nc5 Kb8 16. Be6 Ka8 17. Bd7 Kb8 18. Na6+ Ka8 19. Bc6 mate) **15. Be6+ Kb8 16. Nc5 Ka8 17. Bd7** (wasting a move and mating in two).

Now let's consider Black's alternative:

B: Active Defense

5 ... Kd8 6. Ke6 Kc7 (6 ... Ke8 transposes to the passive line after 7. Nd7, and 6 ... Kc8 creates possibilities similar to the text) **7. Nd7 Kc6** (on other responses White can play the same 8th move) **8. Bd3!** (Black is trapped after all) **8 ... Kc7** (or Kb7) **9. Bb5** (most texts recommend Be4, but Bb5 is more systematic) **9 ... Kd8** (on any other move White plays Kd6) **10. Nb6** (or Nf6) **Kc7 11. Nd5+** (and White has the 2nd net!). A sample conclusion: 11 ... Kd8 12. Kf7 (or Kd6) Kc8 13. Ke7 Kb7 14. Kd7 Kb8 15. Ba6! Ka7 16. Bc8 Kb8 17. Nc3 (or Nb4 or Ne7) 17 ... Ka8 18. Kc7 Ka7 19. Nb5+ Ka8 20. Bb7 mate.

Going back to the starting position (last diagram), here are sample variations showing how White wins if he decides to drive the Black King to h1: 1. Ng6+ Kg8 2. Bd5+ Kh7 3. Be6 Kh6 4. Bg8 Kh5 5. Ne5 and now either *(A)* 5 ... Kh6 6. Ng4+ Kh5 7. Kf5 Kh4 8. Kf4 Kh5 9. Bf7+ Kh4 10. Ne3 Kh3 11. Bg6 Kh4 12. Ng2+ Kh3 13. Kf3 Kh2 14. Kf2 Kh3 15. Bf5+ Kh2 16. Ne3 Khl 17. Bg4 Kh2 18. Nf1+ Kh1 19. Bf3 mate; or *(B)* 5 ... Kh4 6. Kf5 Kg3 7. Ng4 Kf3 8. Bc4 Kg3 9. Be2 Kh4 10. Nf6 Kg3 11. Ne4+ and we've arrived at the 2nd net.

The W Maneuver

A particularly intriguing possibility is the Mahler W maneuver. Although it is not a main line, the W maneuver is worth examining because it shows beautiful interaction among the pieces (and it makes a useful mnemonic device):

DIAGRAM 7

In one satisfying variation all three pieces trace W's: the King by moving over the squares e5, d6, c5, and b6; the Bishop covering d5, c6, b5 and a6; the Knight traversing f4, e6, d4, and c6.
1. Ke5 Kd8 2. Kd6 (tracing the first half of the King's W) **2 ... Ke8 3. Bd5 Kd8 4. Bc6** (the first half of the Bishop's W) **4 ... Kc8 5. Nf4 Kd8** (on 5 ... Kb8 6. Kc5; if then 6 ... Kc7 or Kc8 7. Ne6+ transposes to the main line, and if 6 ... Ka7 7. Kb5 Kb8 8. Kb6 Kc8 9. Ne6 Kb8 10. Bd7 Ka8 11. Nc7+ Kb8 12. Na6+ Ka8 13. Bc6 mate) **6. Ne6+** (the first half of the Knight's W) **6 ... Kc8 7. Kc5 Kb8 8. Kb6** (completing the King's W) **8 ... Kc8** (or Ka8) **9. Bb5 Kb8 10. Ba6** (completing the Bishop's W) **10 ... Ka8 11. Nd4 Kb8 12. Nc6+** (completing the Knight's W) **12 ... Ka8 13. Bb7 mate!**

How to Start

Most of the time your pieces will not be so nicely placed as they are in the analyzed examples, so you need to know how to prepare your forces for action. Unless the position clearly suggests a better plan, start by moving all three pieces to the center; specifically, your King to a central square not the color of your Bishop, the Bishop to a central square next to the King, and the Knight to the other side of the King, so that the three pieces form a straight line (say, Nc4, Kd4, Be4).

This approach is especially helpful when you have no idea what to do. Since a central arrangement can be achieved without much trouble, create random positions and practice trying to centralize the pieces. By grappling with it on your own you should get a better idea of how the pieces work together.

Conclusion

The key patterns that underlie the Bishop-and-Knight mate are strikingly powerful, but they are entirely absent from most text-books. While a single article cannot give you perfect technique, I hope this one at least displays how the Bishop, Knight, and King can function as a unit. I stress this point because interaction is what chess is all about. Never forget that the value of a piece is measured by its relation to other pieces.

6

ROOKS

THE POWERFUL ROOK

This Major Piece Can Be Your Best Friend—If You Know How to Treat It Right

For the novice, no piece is more difficult to handle properly than the Rook. Beginners often fail to bring their Rooks into play during the course of a game—and suffer dire consequences because of it.

Failing to castle is certainly one reason why a Rook never sees action. Also, one needs a little experience to appreciate the need to find and create the open files that provide Rooks with gateways into the thick of it.

Although not as powerful as the Queen, the Rook is stronger than any other piece. Like the Queen, it is powerful enough to demand respect from the enemy King, because it can often threaten to mate or imprison a poorly protected monarch. And unlike the Bishop or Knight, a lone Rook can force checkmate in cooperation with its King. Positions A and B in Diagram 1 show two typical mates with a Rook.

DIAGRAM 1

DIAGRAM 2

Rooks are unique among your pieces because they do not necessarily have greater mobility from the center. No matter where it sits
on an otherwise empty board, a Rook commands fourteen squares.
In position C, the Rooks on a1 and d4 have the same mobility.
Replace the Rooks with any other piece, and the one on d4 will have
greater scope.

Rooks are long-range pieces that often can be more effective from
far away than from up close. At a distance, they can attack without
as much fear of being counterattacked as they would have when
fighting at close quarters. In position D (Diagram 2), for example,
White wants to save his Rooks, which have been forked by Black's
Bishop. White can save his Rooks by first checking at d1 and then
moving the other Rook to safety. In position E, however, 1. Re1+
doesn't work because Black gets out of check with a counterattack
on the checking Rook (1 ... Kf2), still leaving both Rooks vulnerable.

Generally, Rooks should be placed on what we call *open* or *half-
open* files. An open file has no pawns on it; a half-open file contains
pawns of only one color. Rooks use these files as doorways into a
position—sometimes right into the enemy's living room. In position
F (Diagram 3), White will want to place his Rook on the half-open b-
file, and Black will want to shift his Rook to the half-open c-file.

When there are no open or half-open files, you should plan to
make pawn exchanges that will free files for your Rook. You generally have two choices. First, you can search for files with advanced
pawns that might be exchanged. Or, look for files with pawns that
can be pushed forward and exchanged. If your Rooks are already on
the likely files, fine. If not, plan to get them there as soon as
possible. In position G, White could open up the e-file for his Rook
by advancing his pawn to e5 and exchanging it on f6.

DIAGRAM 3   DIAGRAM 4

Sometimes a Rook is brought to an open or half-open file so that it may be transferred elsewhere. This is particularly effective when the Rook seizes the open file with a gain of time. In position H (Diagram 4), White can play 1. Rb1! If Black then defends his b-pawn, he has no adequate answer to 2. Rb3, threatening Rh3 or Rg3.

One way to stop a Rook from using an open file is to oppose it with one of your own. Thus, neither side's Rooks can move freely along the file because of the possibility of capture by the enemy Rook. Therefore, having a Rook on a file is no guarantee you control that file.

But you can strengthen your grip on a file by *doubling* your Rooks; that is, by placing both Rooks (or a Queen and Rook) on the file. Doubled Rooks support each other both in attack and defense. Their combined power can prevent the other side from occupying the same file with Rooks. And the lead Rook, supported by his ally, may be able to break into the enemy camp. In position I (Diagram 5), White's doubled Rooks prevent Black from contesting the c-file. White is ready to invade with 1. Rc7.

It's usually easier to double on a file if your Rook is unopposed (or if you occupy the file first). But even when both sides have one Rook

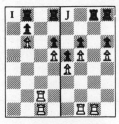

DIAGRAM 5   DIAGRAM 6

on a file, there still are ways to double. In position J (Diagram 5) White can seize the g-file by 1. Rg6! Black has no good options. If he exchanges (1 ... Rxg6), White's recapture (2. fxg6) produces a dangerous supported passed pawn. If Black does nothing, White will double next move with 2. Rfg1.

A major goal of controlling a file is to ultimately scoot a Rook down to the seventh rank, where it may trap the enemy King and thus form the first strand in a mating net. Also, your opponent often has some pawns still resting on their original squares—sitting ducks for your Rook. Even when you can't win material, your invading Rook will often force the enemy's pieces (especially his Rooks) into passivity, for they will be tied down defending unprotected pieces or pawns. In position K (Diagram 6), 1. Rb7 wins a pawn.

Finally, though doubled Rooks can be powerful on a file, imagine what they can do in tandem on the seventh rank. It almost always produces material gain, not to mention strong mating possibilities. In position L, White can mate in three: 1. Rg7+ Kh8 2. Rh7+ Kg8 3. Rdg7 mate.

To find out what Rooks can do through castling, see the article on "Aggressive Safety," page 27.

THE ACTIVE ROOK

The Best Defense May Be a Good Offense

You may not want to play out inferior Rook endings, but now and then you must. Instead of merely defending in such cases, you should try to counterattack and keep your Rook active. In fact, freedom of movement is so important that it is sometimes better to sacrifice a pawn rather than tie down a Rook to its defense.

A classic example of this concept is illustrated in the game Tarrasch-Rubinstein, San Sebastian 1911:

DIAGRAM 1: BLACK TO MOVE

White is already up one pawn and is threatening to win another. Black can protect his b-pawn by either 1 ... Rb8, immobilizing his Rook, or 1 ... Rd6, moving into a precarious pin along White's sixth rank. In response to the latter, White should first play 2. Ke2, guarding his second rank, and then a4-a5, trying to exploit the pin.

Since passive resistance seems quite unpromising, Rubinstein courageously switches to the offensive.

1. ... Rd2!!

Allowing his b-pawn to be captured with check! Perhaps he was prompted by Janowski, who supposedly said that a Rook on the seventh rank is a pig because it eats and eats and eats.

2. Rxb6+ Kg5

Although White has two extra pawns, the Black Rook exerts enough pressure to dissuade White from starting a Queenside advance. On 3. a4 for example, Black forces a draw after 3... f4 4.a5 f3 (threatening a back-rank mate) 5. Ke1 (not 5. h4+ Kg4!—so that the King can hide in front of the White h-pawn—6.Kg1?? Kh3!, with mate to follow) Re2+ 6. Kf1 (not 6. Kd1 because, after 6 ... Rxf2 7.a6 e3 8. a7 Rd2+ 9. Kc1 f2, White wallows in the mud) Rc2 7.Ke1 Re2+. White consequently tries to deal with the menacing Black Rook first.

3. Ke1 Rc2 4. Rb5

White pins the f-pawn to delay the looming avalanche. The natural march of the a-pawn is tempting, but Rubinstein's seventh rank incursion has given Tarrasch second thoughts. Remember that aggressive counteraction is often the surest way to distract the enemy from completing his plans.

4 ... Kg4!

Black breaks the pin and renews the threat to advance the f-pawn.

5. h3 +

Otherwise, Black eats high on the hog after f4 and Kf3.

5 ... Kxh3

Both 5 ... Kf4 and 5 ... Kg5 keep the f-pawn protected but lose valuable time.

6. Rxf5 Rxb2 (chomp) 7. Rf4

Black has nothing to fear from the reasonable alternatives 7. a4 and 7. Rh5 +. In both lines (7. a4 Ra2 8. a5 Kg4 9. Re5 Kf3 and 7. Rh5 + Kg4 8. Rxh7 Rxa2) the position levels out.

7 ... Rxa2 (grunt) 8. Rxe4

White is still a pawn ahead, but Black's active Rook and aggressive King hold the game in dynamic balance.

8 ... h5!

The key to good defense is spirited counterplay. Rubinstein knows that passed pawns must be pushed!

9. c4 Kg2 10. Rf4

Also worth considering is 10. Rh4 for, if Black plays the direct 10 ... Rxf2, White forces a winning King and pawn ending with 11. Rh2 +. One intriguing variation given by Fine continues 11 ... Kxh2 12. Kxf2 h4 13. c5 h3 14. c6 Kh1 15. c7 h2 16. Kg3 (to avoid stalemating Black) Kg1 17. c8 = Q h1 = Q 18. Qc1 mate!

However, Black can still hold if, instead of 10 ... Rxf2, he activates his Rook by 10 ... Ra5! (so that the Rook can annoy the White King along the e-file as well as from the flank). In that case, 11. Ke2 (keeping the pawn protected as he approaches the center) Re5 + 12. Kd3 Kxf2 leads nowhere, while 11. Re4 (to stop the check along the e-file) Ra1 + (notice how the Black Rook is able to function in either direction) 12. Ke2 Ra2 + 13. Ke3 Ra3 + 14. Kd4 Kxf2 15. Rh4 Ra5 obstructs White from making further progress (16. c5 allows Black to win the White Rook with Ra4 +).

10 ... Rc2

To restrain the advance of the c-pawn and illustrating an important principle. Whether defending or attacking, try to place your Rooks behind passed pawns. The point is that, when behind a pawn, the mobility of a Rook increases as the pawn advances.

11. Rh4 Kf6!

Once again, not 11 ... Rxf2 because of 12. Rh2 + !

12. Kd1
White must try something to dislodge the confining Black Rook.
12 ... Rxf2
Just hamming it up.
13. c5 Ke3 14. Rxh5
Although White has managed to stay a pawn ahead, the active Black pieces still offer more than sufficient compensation. Fine neatly points out that 14. c6 wouldn't win either: 14 ... Rf6! 15. c7 (15. Rc4?? drops a Rook because of the mate threat after 15 ... Kd3) 15 ... Rc6, and the pawn falls.
14 ... Kd4
Black will soon win the c-pawn, so they agreed to a draw.

Rubinstein's ingenious handling of this difficult ending shows the value of active resistance as opposed to passive defense. Counterplay is the only way to divert the enemy from his aims, and sacrifice may be necessary to create the attacking chances—especially in Rook endings where mobility is crucial.

To reinforce this lesson, examine the following position for 15 or 20 minutes without moving the pieces. Then write down your ideas, both in words and variations. After recording your thoughts, play through the actual moves and critically compare them to what you've written. (To improve your analysis, Kotov recommends that you do this kind of exercise on a regular basis.)

Finally, if some moves seem unclear, play through an entire example for perspective. An idea should be judged in context, and a move is just one tree in a forest:

DIAGRAM 2: BLACK TO MOVE

The game (Lilienthal-Smyslov, Moscow-Leningrad 1941) concluded:

1 ... g5 2. Rxh7 Rxa2 3. Rh6+ Ke5 4. Rxc6 Ke4 5. Rxc5 f4 6. exf4 Kf3 7. h3 Ra1+

And Black draws, even though he's down four pawns!

THE ACTIVE LIFE

There's No Future for You in Any Game If You've Got a Rook That Isn't Getting the Proper Exercise

There's really no need to extol the virtues of an active Rook. Most rated players seem to know that a Rook can be most effective if it is free to check, threaten, and generally harass; it can sometimes be virtually useless when tied down solely to defense.

Now and then, however, you have no choice but to post a Rook in a purely defensive manner. Sometimes this is done to maintain control of an important line, such as the back rank when the other side threatens mate. Our initial example introduces a set of positions hinging on this type of Rook passivity:

DIAGRAM 1: WHITE TO MOVE

Here is a typical textbook case. White's BP shields his King from check, and his Rook actively patrols the seventh rank. Black's Rook, meanwhile, must stand sentinel on the back row in order to stop mate. It can do no more than mark time. At least Black's King sits in the path of the pawn, guarding the promotion square.

But, even with Black's King so placed, White wins easily. The winning technique is to maneuver the Rook to a8, which mates or snares the hapless Black Rook.

1. Rb7 +.

Not 1. Ra7 at once because 1 ... Rg6 pins the pawn.

1 ... Kc8

After 1 ... Ka8, White continues as in the text.

2. Ra7 Kb8

To guard a8.

3. c7 + Kc8 4. Ra8 +

And White skewers the Rook.

The win with the QP is slightly more complex. Here's an example:

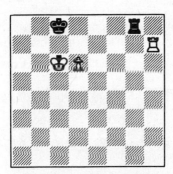

DIAGRAM 2: WHITE TO MOVE

The win is essentially the same as in the previous example, except that the extra file gives Black more room and forces White to play with care.

1. Rc7 +

Here 1. Ra7 accomplishes the same thing.

1 ... Kb8 2. Rb7 + Ka8

Not 2 ... Kc8, losing at once to 3. d7 + followed by 4. Rb8 + .

3. Rb5

The Rook can also move to b4, b3, b2 or b1. In this position, it would be a mistake to advance the pawn right away. After 3. d7, White sets himself up for 3 ... Rg6+ 4. Kc7 Rc6+ (in this variation he could try 4. Kd5 instead, but then must prove he knows how to win the Queen versus Rook ending after 4 ... Kxb7).

After 3. Rb5, White wins by building a bridge (by using his Rook to shield his King from checks).

3 ... Rc8+ 4. Kd7

Here 4. Kd5 eventually wins by the same method.

4 ... Rc1 5. Kd8 Ka7 6. d7 Ka6

This is as reasonable a move as any.

7. Re5

This provides a haven for the King on the e-file, but also playable was 7. Rb8 (or 7. Rd5), with the idea of 8. Rc8.

7 ... Rh1 8. Kc7

Or 8. Ke7.

8 ... Rc1+ 9. Kd6 Rd1+ 10. Rd5

This last move completes the bridge and ensures the pawn's promotion.

With a KP, the win is immediate because the extra file allows White to sneak up behind Black at once by 1. Ra7. The next diagram illustrates this point:

DIAGRAM 3: WHITE TO MOVE

The situation would be different if Black had a slightly more active Rook:

DIAGRAM 4: BLACK TO MOVE

1 ... Ra6 +
Forcing back White's King.
2. Ke5 Ra1!
White's King is unable to find shelter from Black's revitalized Rook. The position is drawn. This last example also shows that the attacking King must be on the sheltered side of the pawn in order to win.

Or consider this:

DIAGRAM 5: BLACK TO MOVE

Even when the defending Rook is on the wrong side of the pawn, sometimes it can become active in surprising ways.

The Black Rook can join the living.
1 ... Re7 +!
There are two points. On 2. dxe7, the game is drawn by stalemate; and, on 2. Kd5, Black plays 2 ... Re2, with endless checks.

As we can see, not all these positions are won. In fact, even when the defending Rook can do no more than guard the back rank, White is unable to win if his pawn is on the Knight or Rook file:

DIAGRAM 6: WHITE TO MOVE

The position is drawn because White doesn't have enough room to operate on the left side of the board.

1. Rb7+ Ka8 2. Ra7+ Kb8

White can't play 3. b7 because of 3 ... Rg6+, winning the Rook and the game.

White could win, however, if he had doubled NPs:

DIAGRAM 7: WHITE TO MOVE

The win is possible here because the extra pawn enables White to swap Rooks while still keeping a pawn on the board.

1. Rh6

151 _____ *Rooks*

It would be wrong to play 1. b7 immediately because 1 ... Rg6+ draws after 2. b6 Rxb6+, as well as after 2. Ka5 Rf6 3. b6 Rf5+ 4. Ka4 (or Ka6) 4 ... Ra5+.
      1 ... Rf8 2. b7 Rg8 3. Rc6 Rh8 4. Rc8+ Rxc8 5. bxc8=Q+ Kxc8 6. Ka7
And the extra pawn decides.

In summary, when the defending King stands in the path of the oncoming pawn, and the defending Rook merely guards against mate on the back rank, the aggressive side *can* win with either a BP or a center pawn—if the pawn, while on the sixth rank, prevents immediate checks to its King.

In cases where the extra pawn is on either the Knight or Rook files, however, Black draws merely by shifting his Rook along the back rank. White doesn't have enough room to perform the winning maneuver.

A GUIDE TO ROOK HANDLING

Two Basic Concepts Guaranteed to Force Rooks into Putting on Their Best Performance

Unlike most theoretical endings, those with Rooks actually arise in everyday play. Moreover, about half of all finales contain these awesome pieces. So, if you have to economize your endgame studies, it makes sense to focus on the basics of Rook endings. In fact, players who really know how to drive these miniature tanks seldom throw away winning games and often salvage hopeless ones, even against stiff opposition.

The following diagram illustrates two of the more fundamental concepts: *bridge building* and *checking distance:*

DIAGRAM 1: WHITE TO PLAY AND WIN
BLACK TO PLAY AND DRAW

Building a Bridge

This technique enables the attacking King to shield itself from checks by the defending Rook. It comes about in the above diagram with White to play.

Notice the pawn is on its seventh rank, the White King is hiding in front and the Black King is cut off from the pawn by one file. If White tries to extricate his King directly by 1. Ke7, Black delivers an unending series of checks: 1 ... Rh7+ 2. Ke6 Rh6+ 3. Kf7 (3. Ke5 or 3. Kd5 meets with 3 ... Rh5+, while 3. Kf5 drops the pawn after 3 ... Rd6) 3 ... Rh7+ 4. Ke8 Rh8+, and so on.

White, of course, helps matters by first driving away the Black King.

1. Rb1+ Ka7

Or 1 ... Ka8 or 1 ... Ka6, but not 1 ... Kc6 because 2. Kc8 wins the Black Rook for the pawn.

But, even with the c-file now clear, White is still unable to free his King without taking further precautions. After 2. Kc7 (2. Ke7 would be met by similar resistance), Black drives back the White monarch by checking along the files: 2 ... Rc2+ 3. Kd6 Rd2+ 4. Kc6 Rc2+ 5. Kb5 (the only way to stop the checks without retreating in front of the pawns) 5 ... Rd2. White consequently must cope with the Black Rook. This is done by positioning the White Rook along its fourth rank so it can block the enemy barrage.

2. Rb4

If the defending King were back on its first rank, 2. Rb5 would also work. But here, 2.Rb5 meets with 2 ... Ka6. (Both 2. Rd1 and 2. Re1 win quickly, but they don't illustrate this useful technique.)

Since 2 ... Rh8+ fails to 3. Kc7, threatening both mate and promotion, Black's best try consists in seizing one of the files.

2 ... Rc2 3. Ke7

Threatening to Queen.

3 ... Re2+ 4. Kd6

Again threatening to Queen.

4 ... Rd2+ 5. Kc6 Rc2+

If Black just temporizes instead, say with 5 ... Rd3, White then plays 6. Rb5. The point is that, with the White King at c6, 6 ... Ka6 would no longer be a threat.

6. Kd5

Threatening once again to Queen.

6 ... Rd2+ 7. Rd4

And the pawn goes through.

Why is it called building a bridge? I could give you a good reason, but I like the one my teacher told me a lot more. He said the White King (here on d5) is Brooklyn and the Black Rook (here on d2) is Manhattan. That's a bridge. Then there's the White Rook that moves from b4 to d4. That's a boat. It was a memorable analogy.

Checking Distance

While White to play in the above diagram wins by building a bridge, Black to play draws by directly attacking the opposing King. This works because the Black Rook has the *checking distance*, which is the minimum distance a Rook needs to be effective (barring unusual tactics, three squares must separate the Rook from its target, in this case the pawn).

In Diagram 1 with Black to move, Black can successfully harass the White King because the checks cannot be stopped without abandoning the pawn.

1 ... Rh8+ 2. Ke7 Rh7+ 3. Ke8 Rh8+ 4. Kf7 Rh7+

Driving the White King back to the pawn. As in an earlier variation, White does no better by moving down the board.

5. Ke6 Rh6+ 6. Kf5

Both 6. Ke5 and 6. Kd5 are answered by 6 ... Rh5+.

6 ... Rd6
Leading to capture of the pawn.

DIAGRAM 2: BLACK TO MOVE

Diagram 2 shows what happens when the Rook does not have the checking distance (that is, when it is not sufficiently distant from its target). Even with the move, Black is now unable to save the game.
1 ... Rh8 + 2. Kf7 Rh7 + 3. Kf8 Rh8 + 4. Kg7
And Black has no more flank checks.
4 ... Ra8
Both 4 ... Rb8 and 4 ... Re8 meet with the same response, while 4 ... Rc8 loses to the text, or also to 5. Rc1 + .
5. Kf7
And Black must sacrifice his Rook for the pawn.
From the second diagram, Black is unable to hold because he doesn't have the checking distance; only two files now separate the Rook from the pawn.
When considering checking distance, be aware that all pawns except those on the a- or h-file have long and short sides (in our first diagram, the short side extends from the a- to the c-file, while the long side goes from the e- to the h-file). Furthermore, the Rook is a long-range piece that works best from far away.
Therefore, if you are defending and your King is cut off from the promotion square, try to post it on the short side of the pawn so that the long side is kept clear for your Rook to give checks.
Otherwise, your Rook will not have the checking distance and, as our second diagram illustrates, that can be fatal.

7

THE QUEEN

TRADING POST

If You're Going to Swap Your Queen for Two Rooks, Be Sure You Know Just What You're Bargaining For

---

Which would you rather have, a Queen or two Rooks? Beginners usually prefer the Queen. They overuse this powerhouse (especially in the opening) and don't appreciate the Rooks enough (sometimes not moving them in the course of an entire game). The answer to "Which would you rather have, a Queen or two Rooks?" depends on another question: "Do the conditions on the board favor the Queen or the Rooks?"

The Queen tends to be stronger when the Rooks are undeveloped, badly placed, or unable to use their power in tandem. In such cases, the multi-talented Queen may be able to fork pieces or execute double attacks, especially when minor pieces (Bishops and Knights) and loose pawns are scattered across the board.

The Rooks get the upper hand when they can use open lines. Then they can often control two adjoining ranks or files, double on the same line, or attack some specific point simultaneously. Since the Queen can defend a particular square only once, Rooks working together can often gobble up material. This frequently leads to a situation where one player captures a pawn knowing that he will have to swap his two Rooks back for the Queen—but that leaves him a pawn up. Thus, in many positions the side with the Queen really needs an extra pawn to keep the game even.

No matter how much two Rooks are worth, whether it's a Queen or a Queen and pawn, you must still understand the conditions that favor each side of the equation.

Rooks are effective when they work in unison. Their ability to control adjoining ranks or files, especially along the board's edge, is a formidable mating force, even against a centralized Queen. This position (Diagram 1) from Sederborg-Spassky (Leningrad 1960) shows how quickly coordinated Rooks can strike. After **1 ... g5+**, White had to resign, for 2. fxg5 hxg5+ either wins the Queen or mates (3. Kh5 Rxh3).

DIAGRAM 1: BLACK TO MOVE   DIAGRAM 2: BLACK TO MOVE

If the enemy King is trapped on the edge by one of the two Rooks (accomplished by posting a Rook on the adjoining rank or file), the other Rook may provide dangerous mating threats. Fischer-Tal (Bled 1961) illustrates that, even when the Queen stops the mate, it can sometimes be won by sacrificing one Rook to set up a devastating skewer (Diagram 2). Here, 1 ... Qxg4 loses the Queen after 2. Rh1 (threatening mate) 2 ... Qd4 3. Rh8+! Qxh8 4. Rb8+.

Sometimes one Rook is sacrificed so that the other can be exchanged for the Queen, simplifying to a winning endgame. In Diagram 3, Petrosian-Mikenas (Kiev 1957), White swaps down to an easy win with **1. Rxg5 +! Qxg5 + 2. Rg4,** pinning the Queen.

DIAGRAM 3: WHITE TO MOVE   DIAGRAM 4: BLACK TO MOVE

An effective way to use Rooks is to double them on the same line, so that in both attack and defense they are twice as strong. The most potent tactic is to double on the seventh rank, as in this position from Mikhalchisin-Kasparov (Moscow 1981). White resigned here (Diagram 4) after the crushing 1 ... Rff2, when he must trade down to a losing endgame to avoid deadly threats.

The Queen generally gets the best of it when the Rooks can't cooperate. In such cases, the Queen can often perform as if the Rooks don't exist. A vulnerable enemy King can be virtually undefendable if the Queen can combine with other forces, as in Fischer–Saidy (Log Cabin 30–30 1957). White in Diagram 5 would have won easily with 1. Qh6. If the undefended Bishop moves along the a1-h8 diagonal, 2. Nc7 is mate; if the Bishop shifts along the d8-h4 diagonal, 2 Qg7 is mate.

When the Rooks are poorly placed and there are minor pieces on the board, the Queen can sometimes generate irresistible threats that force the side with the Rooks to sacrifice material to break the attack. In Bogolubov–Alekhine (Hastings 1922), for example (Diagram 6), 1 ... Bb5 was so strong that White had no choice but to surrender the Exchange by 2. Rxb5, for 2. Nd2 Qc1 3. Rxb5 Nf3 + 4. Kg2 Qg1 + 5. Kh3 Qxh2 is mate.

DIAGRAM 5: WHITE TO MOVE   DIAGRAM 6: BLACK TO MOVE

If the Rooks are uncoordinated, they can get into trouble trying to stop the advance of a menacing passed pawn. In Huebner–Ljubojevic (Tilburg 1979), White's Queen was able to discombobulate

DIAGRAM 7: WHITE TO MOVE

Black after **1. Qg4** (Diagram 7). Although the material is roughly balanced, White's Queen and passed pawn proved too strong after **1 ... Kd7 2. h6 Ke7** (2 ... Rh8 3. Qd4 Rxh6 loses to 4. Qg7 +) **4. Qd4 Rf6 5. Qe5 + Re6 6. h7.**

Ordinarily, the Rooks are equal to a Queen and pawn. When the position slightly favors the Queen, the Rooks should be poised for counterattack. Sometimes the defender can draw by doubling his Rooks along a key line, thus stopping passed pawns and King invasions while keeping weak points guarded. In such cases, the draw is often secured by simply shuffling one or both Rooks along the same row they occupy.

If the position slightly favors the Rooks, the Queen might draw by threatening to give perpetual check. Unless permanent shelter can be found for the harassed King, there may be no way to avoid the draw.

Occasionally, the position favors neither the Queen or the Rooks. It actually favors three minor pieces, but that's another article.

OF QUEENS AND PAWNS

Your Queen Can Beat a Single Pawn Any Day, Right? Don't Count on It!

A very useful ending to know is Queen versus pawn on the seventh rank, defended by the King. It usually arises after one side wins the race to Queen by two moves. While it is generally thought the Queen wins automatically, the pawn actually draws about 45 percent of the time.

Clearly the Queen stops the pawn if it can occupy the promotion square, but the decisive factors tend to be more subtle. The result can depend on:

- The kind of pawn.
- The closeness of the attacking King.
- The ability of the Queen to start with a check or a pin.

The Basic Method

The winning process consists in moving the Queen closer and closer to the pawn, often by a zigzagging series of checks, threats and pins, until the defending King must protect the pawn by moving in front of it. The attacking King can then capitalize on the pawn's temporary obstruction by moving a square closer. The obstruction process is repeated as many times as necessary, until the attacking King is close enough to support mate or to help win the pawn.

DIAGRAM 1

Queen vs. Center Pawn

This is always a win unless the Queen can't start with a check or a pin. In the diagram above, White has several ways to start the winning procedure, the most compelling being ...

1. Qf4+

Play might then continue:

1 ... Kg2

Not 1 ... Ke1, voluntarily blocking the pawn. And 1 ... Kg1 would be answered as in the text.

2. Qe3 Kf1 3. Qf3+

Forcing the King in front of the pawn.

3 ... Ke1 4. Kb7

White can do this because Black's pawn is blocked.

4 ... Kd2

Notice that 4 ... Kd1 leaves the pawn pinned.

5. Qf2

This is faster than checking at d5, while the check at f4 is quick enough but less consistent with the plan we are pursuing.

5 ... Kd1 6. Qd4+ Kc2

Once again, 6 ... Ke1 blocks the pawn, and 6 ... Kc1 is answered as in the text.

7. Qe3 Kd1 8. Qd3+ Ke1 9. Kc6 Kf2 10. Qd2 Kf1

Of course 10 ... Kf3 loses to 11. Qe1.

11. Qf4+ Kg2 12. Qe3 Kf1 13. Qf3+ Ke1 14. Kd5 Kd2 15. Qf2 Kd1 16. Qd4+ Kc2 17. Qe3 Kd1 18. Qd3+ Ke1 19. Ke4 Kf2 20. Qf3+ Ke1 21. Kd3 Kd1 22. Qxe2+

And mate next move.

DIAGRAM 2

Diagram 2 is the only way a center pawn can draw (White's King could also be at f5 or f6). Since the Queen can't start with a pin, and since White's own King obstructs checks along the f-file, the pawn's advance can't be stopped.

DIAGRAM 3

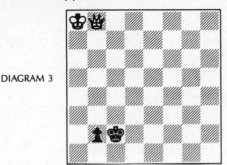

Queen vs. Knight Pawn

This should be a win if the Queen has the first move. The winning method is faster here because the lack of space forces the King to block its pawn more frequently. Play might continue:

1. Qc7 + Kd2 2. Qb6
Or 2. Qd6 + .
2 ... Kc2 3. Qc5 + Kd2 4. Qb4 +
Or 4. Qd4 + .
4 ... Kc2 5. Qc4 + Kd2 6. Qb3 Kc1 7. Qc3 +
Notice how the Queen has zigzagged up the board.
7 ... Kb1 8. Kb7 Ka2 9. Qc2 Ka1 10. Qa4 +
Here the lack of room forces the King to block its pawn prematurely.
10 ... Kb1 11. Kc6 Kc1 12. Qc4 + Kd2 13. Qb3 Kc1 14. Qc3 + Kb1 15. Kb5
Or 15. Kc5.
15 ... Ka2 16. Qc2
Less consistent but better is 16. Ka4! since, if 16 ... b8 = Q, then White mates by 17.Qa3!.
16 ... Ka1 17. Qa4 + Kb1 18. Kc4
Or 18. Kb4.
18 ... Kc1 19. Kc3 b1 = Q
Not 19 ... Kb1, which loses to 20. Qc2 + , while 19 ... b8 = N + is only good for a laugh.
20. Qf4 + Kd1 21. Qd2 mate.

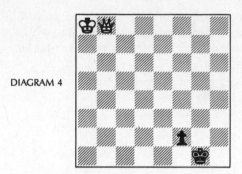

DIAGRAM 4

Queen vs. Bishop Pawn

This ending is drawn unless the attacking King is within striking distance. The defending King cannot be forced to block its pawn but instead retreats to the corner; the threat of stalemate leaves the pawn safe from capture.

If, in the above position, White plays 1. Qg3 +, Black doesn't have to block his pawn by 1 ... Kf1, but can safely abandon it by 1 ... Kh1, maintaining the threat to advance. The point is that 2. Qxf2 is stalemate. The necessary conditions under which a Bishop-pawn can be beaten are illustrated in this position:

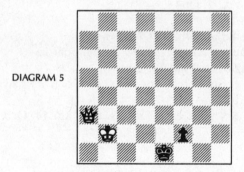

DIAGRAM 5

White to play can win because his King is already close enough to inflict real damage and because the Black King can be prevented from reaching the short side of the pawn, where a stalemate is possible. Correct is ...

1. Qg3!

Pinning the pawn and cutting off the Black King.

1 ... Ke2
Not 1 ... Kf1, which freely allows the White King an extra tempo.
2. Qg2!
To mate at d2 if Black promotes.
2 ... Ke1 3. Kc2
This is better than 3. Kc3 because, in some positions, there's a mate at d1 if that square is guarded by the King.
3 ... Ke2
Forced, since 3 ... f1 = Q allows 4. Qd2 mate.
4. Qe4 + Kf1 5. Qg4! Ke1 6. Qd1 mate.

DIAGRAM 6

Queen vs. Rook Pawn

Here's a case where the Rook pawn seems to be made of sterner stuff. This ending is usually drawn because the defending King is threatened by stalemate after being forced in front of the pawn. The White King accordingly doesn't have the time to move closer.

Here 1. Qg3 + is answered by 1 ... Kh1. Since this is the best White can do, the game is drawn.

The only way a Rook pawn can lose is if the attacking King can get close enough to support mate, either before or after promotion. The next diagram shows a case where the attacking King is much closer than it appears:

DIAGRAM 7

Believe it or not, White wins with ...
1. Kg6
Staying on the g-file to avoid stalemate.
1 ... Kg2
Or 1 ... Kg1.
2. Kh5 +
Or 2.Kf5 +.
2 ... Kf2 3. Qd5
Several other moves also win, but this is best.
3 ... Kg1 4. Qd1 + Kg2
Not 4 ... Kf2 because of 5. Qh1.
5. Qe2 + Kg1 6. Kh4!
This is flashier than 6. Kg4.
6 ... h1 = Q 7. Kg3
And, Black can't avoid mate.

Generally Speaking

In summary we see that Knight and center pawns normally lose, unless the Queen can't start with a pin or a check, whereas Bishop and Rook pawns usually draw, unless the attacking King is close enough to negate the threat of stalemate.

It is noteworthy here that the Rook pawn, ordinarily the weakest of all chessmen, turns out to have more drawing power than its central counterpart. Maybe there's a lesson in this. Although we know better, we tend to treat principles too absolutely. This can backfire because, under the right conditions, the opposite of a principle may be one itself. The keynote is flexibility.

ROYAL HEADACHES

The Lament of the Outfoxed: 'My Kingdom for a Queen!'

Unless you can easily see long sequences of checks and threats, unless you are Bobby Fischer, Mr. Spock, or an H.A.L.-9000 computer, you may have trouble with Queen endgames. Fraught with surprising pitfalls and unexpected shots, these endgames can be extremely tactical—and tricky.

A key problem is that the Queen's sudden striking power makes it difficult for an opposing King to avoid nasty checks while trying to become active. Yet, there often is no choice: A King may have to take part in the attack or support its advancing pawns.

Moreover, sometimes the King must head right into the teeth of the enemy Queen in order to escape it. This startling twist may work because, as a King approaches the other side of the board, a friendly pawn and Queen might be able to set up a zone of safety where no checks are possible, or where the only available check can be answered by a shielding cross-check and a trade of Queens.

Although these endgames should be played very carefully, your task can be simplified by remembering one general idea. You can limit the power of the enemy Queen by centralizing your own. Many Queen endgames actually hinge on this point. Consider the position in the diagram below.

Material is even. Black seems to stand well because his d-pawn looks menacing and his Queen appears poised for action. On reflection, however, the d-pawn isn't really going anywhere yet, and the Queen can be driven from her catbird seat (see Move 1).

DIAGRAM 1: WHITE TO MOVE

Analyze further, and you may also detect just how little cover the Black pawns provide their King. If White ever had to, he probably could squeeze a draw by perpetual checks and threats. White, meanwhile, can find uncheckable shelter for his King at h2 because his Queen controls the vital h2-b8 diagonal. In addition to these clear advantages, White has the move.

1. b4!

This deflecting jab wins the d-pawn, for the Black Queen can no longer guard it and stave off mate (observe that the White Queen eyes f8). White could have won the a-pawn instead but, after 1. Qb8+ Kg7 2. Qxa7+ Kf6 (or Kh6), Black is not only threatening to draw by pendulum checks at c1 and f4, but he also retains his ace-in-the-hole, the passed d-pawn. Besides, by winning this potential monster, the White Queen assumes a central post.

1 ... Qc8

Black abandons the pawn at once, but no better was 1 ... Qd5, since, after 2. Qf8+ Qg8 3. Qf6+ Qg7 4. Qd8+ Qg8 5. Qxd4+, White trades down to a won King-and-pawn endgame. A typical continuation might then be 5 ... Qg7 6. Qxg7+ Kxg7 7. f4 (pushing the unopposed pawn first) 7 ... Kf6 8. Kf2 Kf5 (8 ... g5 makes it easier for White to create a passed pawn) 9. Kf3 h5? (the defender should avoid weakening pawn moves unless he has good and clear reasons) 10. g4+ hxg4 11. hxg4+ Kf6 (or 11 ... Ke6) 12. Ke4 Ke6 13. f5+ gxf5+ (after 13 ... Kf6 White captures on g6 and then cleans up the Queenside) 14. gxf5+ Kf6 15. Kf4 Kf7 16. Ke5 Ke7, and now White can win either by ditching his f-pawn and gobbling the Queenside pawns, or by showing some humor with 17. b5 Kf7 18. f6 Kf8 19. Ke6 Ke8 20. f7+ Kf8 21. Kf6! a5 (or a6) 22. bxa6 b5 23. a7 and mate next.

2. Qxd4+ Kg8

The real endgame begins now. White has the following advantages: the move, invasion squares for his King (g5, f6, h7), an extra pawn in a three-to-two Kingside majority, and a commanding Queen.

From the center, the White Queen hampers its enemy counterpart, watches over its own King and pawns, and directs the thrust into the Black heartland.

3. a4

White intends to secure his pawns by placing them on a4 and b5, after which his dominant Queen stands sentinel over both flanks.

3 ... Qc7

Black correctly assumes a waiting policy and safeguards his second rank, which is especially vulnerable since it contains the bases of both pawn chains.

4. b5 Kf7 5. f4!

Remember Capablanca's rule: When mobilizing a pawn majority, start by moving the unopposed pawn—the one that is likely to become passed because it has no enemy pawns in front of it on the same file.

5 ... Ke6

Black continues to show good judgment. Instead of making irreparable pawn moves, he realigns his pieces, hoping for White to overextend himself.

6. Kf2

White plans to trek his monarch to the weakened enemy Kingside before the final offensive.

6 ... Kf7 7. Kg3 h5?

DIAGRAM 2

Even though this seizes g4, it irreversibly weakens the Kingside (g6 is far easier to attack than h7). Furthermore, Black can no longer guard g5 with a pawn and will find it harder to keep out the White King.

Nonetheless, the imperious White Queen ensures that even prudent defense shouldn't hold this position. For example, after 7 ... Ke6 8. Kg4 Kf7 9. Qd5 + (to reposition the Queen for the next stage) 9 ... Kf8 [forced because 9 ... Ke8, Ke7 and Kg7 all allow White to trade Queens by Qe5 +, while 9 ... Kf6 loses to 10. Qc6 + Qxc6 11. bxc6 Ke6 12. Kg5 a5 (12 ... a6 saves a pawn but loses a tempo) 13. g4 b5 14. f5 + gxf5 15. gxf5 + Kd6 16. f6 enables White to Queen first] 10. Qe5 (offering a Queen trade and threatening Qh8 + followed by Qxh7 +) 10 ... Qd7 + 11. Kg5 (and now, if 11 ... Qd8 +, then White has the cross-check 12. Qf6 +, simplifying to a won King and pawn endgame) 11 ... Kg8 (to stop 12. Qh8 +) 12. g4 Qd8 + 13. Qf6 (but not 13. Kh6?? because of 13 ... Qh4 +—this is what I mean about tricky Queens), and the invasion of the White pieces should prove decisive.

8. Qd5 + Kf8

This move is forced, as in the previous note. After 8 ... Kf6, for example, play might continue 9. Qc6 + Qxc6 10. bxc6 Ke6 11. Kh4 a5 (11 ... Kd6 12. Kg5 followed by Kxg6, promoting the f-pawn) 12. g4 b5 13. f5 + gxf5 14. gxf5 + Kd6 (14 ... Kxf5 loses to 15. c7) 15. f6, and White will Queen two moves ahead of Black.

9. Qe5 Qf7 10. Kh4 Kg8

Black wants to redeploy his King to h7 to keep out the enemy King after it reaches g5. Notice how the central White Queen reigns over the board and helps its own King invade.

11. Kg5 Kh7 12. f5

DIAGRAM 3: BLACK RESIGNS

Black really has no way to prevent an exchange of Queens without incurring immediate loss. The comical 12 ... Qg8, for example, loses after 13. Qe7 + Kh8 14. Kh6, threatening death and worse along the a1-h8 diagonal. White had an extra pawn throughout, but an extra pawn isn't always decisive.

The defending Queen can make these endings quite treacherous. This is especially true because the attacking King might have to risk taking part in the fight. As the above example illustrates, you can minimize the danger of counterattack by placing your Queen in the center (unless you clearly see a better plan).

And don't let your Queen be lured from the center to win a meaningless pawn, unless you're eager to start the next game right away.

8

THE KING

OPPOSITES REPEL

In a Direct Confrontation Between Kings, the Kingdom Is Often Won By the Monarch Who Moves *Second*

In general, the King seems to be a weak piece. As the focus of the other side's attack, it's often quite vulnerable, and in the opening and middlegame, when most pieces are still on the board, the King needs protection from the enemy. But the same King as a fighting piece has admirably strong qualities, for it can attack or guard all immediately adjacent squares. Particularly in the endgame, when it is less likely that it will fall victim to a sudden mate or tactical snare, the King may play an active role.

Kings can march across the board, assail weaknesses, clear traffic for passed pawns, stop invasions, guard key squares, and even help set up mating threats. Advantages gained from an active King in the endgame usually outweigh the risks of exposing it to potential threats.

When both Kings get involved, they may actually square off head to head. This duel might determine the outcome of the game. The term signifying the struggle between the two Kings to achieve dominance is the *opposition*. Diagram 1 illustrates the concept in its purest form. Neither side can win this position, but it's still possible to talk of King superiority (in fact, with no other forces on the board, the concept is easier to understand). Which King stands better?

The answer depends on whose move it is. As it turns out, whoever goes *second* has the advantage. If White goes first, he can play his King to any of five squares: d4, f4, d3, e3, or f3. Whatever White does, Black has a strong response. Retreating to the third rank allows Black's King to move up on White (1. Kd3 is met by 1 ... Kd5, 1. Ke3 by 1 ... Ke5, and 1. Kf3 by 1 ... Kf5). No better is 1. Kd4, moving to the side and presenting Black with an option. Black can either hold the fort with 1 ... Kd6, stopping White from heading up the board, or play more aggressively with 1 ... Kf5, advancing on White. Similarly, 1. Kf4 can be answered by the defensive-minded 1 ... Kf6 or the offensive 1 ... Kd5, turning up the board. (When one King sidesteps his opposite number this way, it's called a *turning maneuver*.)

Regardless of what White plays, Black gets the advantage by going second. That seems unimportant in this setting, but in endgames it is a crucial factor. The real point here is that Black has all the options; he can prevent White from advancing, or he can advance into White's position while White looks on helplessly.

If it were Black who goes first, White would determine the course of play by moving according to the above analysis. Whoever goes first is in *zugzwang*, a German word referring to a situation where, by moving, one must worsen his position (so he prefers not to move). It's thus obviously advantageous to move second, waiting for your opponent to give ground.

DIAGRAM 1

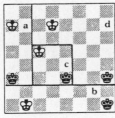

DIAGRAM 2A–2D   DIAGRAM 3

In such positions, the player moving second is said to "have the opposition." If you have the opposition, you "have the advantage" (the terms are virtually synonymous). Kings stand in opposition if they are separated by an odd number of squares along the same rank, file, or diagonal. The type of opposition illustrated in the first diagram is called *direct opposition*. If this condition is fulfilled, the Kings must occupy squares of the same color.

Other types of opposition are illustrated in Diagram 2a–d. In (a) and (b), the Kings stand in *distant opposition*, separated along the same row by three and five squares respectively. In (c) and (d), they are in *diagonal opposition*, separated along the same diagonal by one and three squares. In all four cases, whoever doesn't have the move has the opposition and the advantage. Whoever has the move is in *zugzwang* and must give ground. Looking at it another way, if you have the opposition in such instances, you can ultimately prevent the enemy King from advancing along the occupied row. Thus in (a), if White approaches with 1. Ka6, Black can stop further advances along the a-file by 1 ... Ka4.

Rectangular opposition (also known as *oblique opposition*) is the only opposition where Kings do not have to occupy the same straight row of squares. However, the Kings must still occupy squares of the same color. How do you determine if Kings on different rows stand in this type of opposition? Box off in your mind the smallest possible rectangle containing the two pieces. If both the long and short sides of the rectangle are odd in number (five and three squares in Diagram 3), and if the Kings occupy squares of the same color, they are in rectangular opposition, and whoever doesn't move has the advantage. If either side of the rectangle has an even number of squares, or the Kings occupy squares of different colors, they are not in opposition.

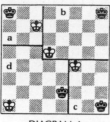

DIAGRAM 4   DIAGRAM 5

When the Kings don't stand in opposition on an otherwise empty board, whoever is on move has the advantage, because he can shift his own King into opposition, forcing his opponent to move. Diagram 4 shows four examples of *seizing the opposition* when the Kings do not already stand in opposition. In (a), White can take either the direct opposition (1. Kc8) or the diagonal opposition (1. Kc6). Black to play could seize the direct opposition by 1 ... Ka7. In (b) White can move into rectangular opposition with 1. Kd6, while Black to play can do it with 1 ... Kh7. White takes the diagonal opposition (1. Kf3) in (c), or if it's Black's turn, 1 ... Kh2 gives him the advantage. In (d), whoever goes first takes the distant opposition. White by 1. Ka2 and Black by 1 ... Ke1.

The most basic occurrence of the opposition with pawns on the board is shown in Diagram 5. Whoever doesn't move has the opposition. If White has it, he wins, for Black moves first and gives way: 1 ... Kb8 2. b7 Ka7 3. Kc7, and White's pawn Queens on the next move. If Black has the opposition, the game is drawn, for if White tries to force through his passed pawn he gives stalemate: 1. b7+ Kb8 2. Kb6. In this example, neither player wants to move.

We have considered the opposition mainly in its abstract sense, with no pawns on the board. But actually, the concept has great practical value and is often the key to solving complicated endings. It is the tool Kings use in their fight to occupy important squares. Once you understand this, your endgame should really start to improve. You may even realize the King is a powerful piece. Use it!

KEEPING YOUR DISTANCE

The Pawn Is on the Run, and You're Out to Catch It. Here's an Easy Way to Figure Out Who Wins the Race

When analyzing endgame positions it's often more efficient to apply rules of thumb than to calculate variations. Of all the time-saving tools in the chessplayer's arsenal, the "square of the pawn" is one of the most basic. This shortcut involves visualizing a set of squares in such a way that it can be determined at a glance whether a defending King can overtake a passed pawn before it Queens. If the King can move into the imagined zone, or is already in it, the pawn can be caught; if the King can't do this, the pawn Queens. It's as simple as that.

Note the expression "square of the pawn" does not refer to the actual square the pawn occupies, but to a larger area containing a group of ordinary squares arranged in a block.

To ascertain the square of the pawn, start by drawing a mental vector from the square the pawn occupies (and including it) to the square of promotion (and including that). This line constitutes the side of the geometric square that you should complete in your head.

In Diagram 1, for example, the square of the pawn goes from a5 to a8 to d8 to d5 to a5 and comprises the 16 squares enclosed in that delineated quadrant. If the defending King can occupy any of the regular squares within that region (in the above case, if it can reach a5, a6, a7, a8, b8, b7, b6, b5, c5, c6, c7, c8, d8, d7, d6 or d5) it can stop the pawn.

In our first position, Black to move draws because he can play 1 ... Kd5, entering the cordoned territory. If it were White's turn to play, the advance 1. a6 would reduce the size of the square, making it impossible for the Black King to catch the pawn. A familiar problem touching upon this theme is Reti's immortal *diagonal march,* one of the most simple and elegant compositions in all of chess literature:

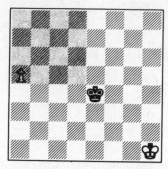

DIAGRAM 1: BLACK TO MOVE   DIAGRAM 2: WHITE TO MOVE

White's situation (Diagram 2) seems hopeless. It doesn't appear he can either catch the Black pawn or defend his own in time. Yet, by moving his King back along the a1-h8 diagonal, White can threaten both actions simultaneously, diverting Black just enough to save the game. For example:

1. Kg7

Now Black can either go for the White pawn or advance his own.

1 ... Kb6 2. Kf6

Threatening to win the Black pawn by penetrating the square g5.

2 ... h4 3. Ke5!

Again threatening to enter the pawn's square, but this time at f4 or e4. A logical conclusion might then be:

3 ... h3 4. Kd6

Securing his own pawn.

4 ... h2 5. c7 h1 = Q 6. c8 = Q

It's a clear draw because, even with the move, Black can't force mate or win the White Queen. If, instead of 1 ... Kb6, Black tries ...

1 ... h4

...the position still leads to a draw.

2. Kf6 h3

Here 2 ... Kb6 only transposes into the first line after 3. Ke5.

3. Ke6 h2 4. c7 h1 = Q 5. c8 = Q +

White fortunately Queens with check.

The leitmotif of this kind of example is whether the defending King can get back in time just by traveling along the diagonal leading to the promotion square. This key line is generally known as the *critical diagonal of retreat*. One class of endgame problems revolves around obstructing this important avenue so that the defending King can't catch the pawn even if it can get within the perimeter of the square:

DIAGRAM 3: WHITE TO MOVE

In the above problem by Bianchetti, White should not proceed directly by advancing his passed pawn for, after 1. a4 Ke4 2. a5 Kd5, the a-pawn falls. To win, White must first block the critical diagonal of retreat. Correct is:

1. d5

Play might continue:

1 ... exd5 2. a4 d4 3. a5 d3 4. Ke1

Having dealt with the Black pawn, White can now safely move in for the Queen.

Sometimes you can counter a line-blocking sacrifice by shifting your King to another diagonal without losing time. To do this, you will have to gain a move by threatening to do something else with your King, as in the following example from a game between Emanuel Lasker and Siegbert Tarrasch:

DIAGRAM 4: WHITE TO MOVE

Lasker's task here seems insurmountable. If he tries 1. Kf6, Black wins with 1 ... c4, for after 2. bxc4 (equally fruitless would be 2.Ke5 c3 3.bxc3 a4) 2 ... bxc4 3.Ke5 c3 4.bxc3 a4, the obstructed diagonal would prevent the White King from reaching the promotion square fast enough. Nevertheless, Lasker was able to avoid the losing cul-de-sac by first threatening to save his h-pawn with ...

1. Kg6

The surprising feint gave White the time to shift his King to a diagonal that couldn't be blocked (namely, the line b1-h7). From there, Lasker's King had no difficulty getting back soon enough to hold the fort.

The feint and the diagonal march, tactics and strategy: Terms like these imply a relationship between chess and the military. Emanuel Lasker himself believed that battle plans sketched on the ground inspired the invention of board games. And it's true; many professional soldiers do enjoy a good Kingside assault. On the other hand, I've never wanted to attack France.

OUTFLANKING IN THE ENDGAME

Some Kings Are More Equal Than Others When Two Pawns Face Off

A common endgame situation is King and pawn against King and pawn. When the pawns are on the same file and immobilized (or fixed), a certain maneuver is often available by which one King is able to force the other one away from the pawns. The term "outflanking" has been used to describe this maneuver.

A striking position from Nimzovich's *My System* will illuminate the idea:

WHITE TO PLAY AND WIN

It seems, superficially, that Black can hardly lose: his King appears to be better placed than White's. Unfortunately for Black, however, his King's mobility is severely restricted by White's pawn.

White should play 1. Kb7, giving Black two choices: to mark time and defend his pawn or to attack White's pawn. If he defends, he loses the pawn and the game: 1 ... Ke7 2. Kc7 Ke8 3. Kd6 Kf7 4. Kd7. White wins because Black's pawn can be attacked from both d6 and d7 but can be defended only from f7. The attacker's extra tempo is decisive—Black is outflanked.

If Black counterattacks instead, a likely sequence is 1 ... Kg6 2. Kc6 Kg5 (2 ... Kf5 3. Kd6 wins) 3. Kd7 Kf5 4. Kd6 winning. The final position illustrates a true mutual *zugzwang*—neither player wants to move, but since Black must move, he loses.

Remember outflanking can occur only if pawns are fixed and one King can outmaneuver the other (because key squares are blocked or guarded). Let's look at another example to solidify our view of the concept:

WHITE TO PLAY AND WIN

Even though his King is far from the main theater, White is able to outflank Black by 1. Kg3 Kb7 2. Kf4 Kc7 3. Ke5 Kd7 4. Kd5 Kc7 5. Ke6 Kc8 6. Kd6 Kb7 7. Kd7 Kb8 8. Kc6 Ka7 9. Kc7. That White should win from the starting position seems almost unlawful! You've probably had this kind of position in your own games and thought nothing of it.

Outflanking Doesn't Always Win

Though outflanking may win a pawn, this doesn't necessarily win the game. The following positions will clarify this point:

WHITE TO PLAY
WINS

WHITE TO PLAY
DRAWS

In the diagram on the left Black loses—even though he temporarily has the opposition—after 1. Kb6 Kb8 2. c6 Kc8 3. c7. In the diagram on the right he draws—because he can *maintain* the opposition—after 1. Kb5 Kb7 2. c5 Kc7 3. c6 Kc8 4. Kb6 Kb8.

Remember: to outflank *and win* you must capture the enemy pawn on either its second or third rank; the capture on any other rank enables the defending King to draw by taking and holding the opposition. The next diagram illustrates this distinction:

BLACK TO PLAY
AND DRAW

If Black tries the reasonable-looking 1 ... Kb7, White creates a favorable outflanking situation with 2. b5! (for instance, 2 ... Kc7 3. Ke6 Kc8 4. Kd6 Kb7 5. Kd7 Kb8 6. Kc6 Ka7 7. Kc7 Ka8 8. Kxb6 Kb8 9. Ka6 Ka8 10. b6 Kb8 11. b7). Black will lose the pawn anyway, but the rank on which the pawn stands when it is taken is crucial. Therefore Black should play the timely 1 ... b5!; even though White still wins the pawn, Black will be able to seize—and maintain—the opposition and draw after 2. Kc5 Ka7 3. Kxb5 Kb7. As we see, the defender himself can capitalize on a knowledge of the outflanking maneuver.

Outflanking Disguised

Sometimes an outflanking possibility is camouflaged and therefore overlooked. The following pawn endgame reveals an unexpected outflanking resource:

WHITE TO PLAY AND WIN

King moves lead White nowhere, for Black can hold the opposition when it counts. Instead of aimless shifting, White should immediately sacrifice the f-pawn to clear f6 for the King, and then outflank. As indicated in Capablanca's *Chess Fundamentals*, White wins after 1. f7! Kxf7 2. Kd6 Kf8 3. Ke6 Kg7 4. Ke7 Kg8 5. Kf6 Kh7 6.Kf7.

The transformation of a material advantage in the endgame into a favorable outflanking situation is often a key step in the winning process. Examine the following position carefully, for it too conceals an outflanking maneuver:

BLACK TO PLAY AND WIN

Black, it seems, has only two ideas to consider: to play for mate or to eventually trade Rook for Bishop and pawn. Knowledge of outflanking, however, would enable Black to find a third path instantly: he should convert his material advantage into an outflanking win by the immediate 1 ... Rxf3! 2. gxf3 Kd4. Surprisingly, this elementary transaction was missed by a group of five analysts, including two experts, two masters, and a USCF senior master!

Next we see a variation of a standard textbook position:

WHITE TO PLAY AND WIN

A first glance suggests that a lengthy endgame cannot be avoided. Surely White will need a long series of subtle moves to win this one. But instead of intricate maneuvers to find the "right" position, White can win at once with 1. Qxd6+! cxd6 2. Kf6 (outflanking). You'd better look at this one again.

Our final problem is taken from a Yugoslav endgame text that merely gives the solution, not the concept:

WHITE TO PLAY AND WIN

The obvious try—to sacrifice the Knight for Black's pawn—fails: 1. Ke5 Kb7 2. Nxc7 Kxc7 3. Kd5 Kd7. The sure path to victory is to establish a winning outflanking structure: 1. Nb6 + ! cxb6 (if 1 ... Kb7 2. Nc4 wins) 2. Ke5 Kc7 (2 ... Kd7 3. Kd5 transposes) 3. Ke6 and White outflanks!

Conclusion

In one sense, we have explored outflanking, an important but neglected concept applying to Kings and pawns. In a larger sense, however, this article is really about the superficial way we examine "ordinary" chess positions. Generally, we miss elementary possibilities because they are slightly hidden or unexpected—and because we have never considered them in proper context. Some of the blame must fall on chess literature. Still, if we judge each position objectively—as if it were unique—we might just discover the obvious.

GOING IN CIRCLES

If at First It Doesn't Correspond, Try Triangulation

Although the Queen can also do it, triangulation is mainly a King maneuver that applies to pure King and pawn endgames. The purpose of this maneuver is to enable an attacking King to break a correspondence between itself and a defending King, without changing the position, thus shifting the burden of having to make a move to the other side. In other words, it is a way to lose a move, to force the other side into moving when it doesn't want to.

It is called *triangulation* because the attacking King often traces a triangle in its movement while trying to set up a *zugzwang* situation (*zugzwang* is a condition where having to play a move is undesirable). The following position is a case in point:

DIAGRAM 1

Black loses here if it's his turn to play. For example, if he starts with 1 ... Kc7, White plays 2. Kc5. Black then has to retreat his King, allowing the White monarch to invade on b6. This wins the a-pawn and ultimately the game.

If Black instead tries 1 ... Kd8 (or 1 ... Kb8), White takes the opposition with 2. Kd6 and soon Queens the c-pawn. After 2 ... Kc8, play might continue 3. c7 Kb7 4. Kd7 Ka7 5. Kc6 (so as to Queen with check, avoiding the stalemate after 5. c8 = Q) 5 ... Ka8 6. c8 = Q + Ka7 7. Qb7 mate.

So Black to play clearly loses. On the other hand, what happens if it's White's turn to move?

If White immediately tries to reach b6 with 1. Kc5, Black forestalls the incursion by 1 ... Kc7. Alternatively, if White tries to make headway with 1. Kd6, Black seizes the direct opposition by 1 ... Kd8, and once again halts the White advance. (It would be a mistake to continue with 2. c7+, for after 2 ... Kc8, White will have to abandon his pawn or give stalemate by 3. Kc6.)

Our exploration so far has led us to two superficial conclusions: White to play draws, and Black to play loses.

The above reasoning suggests a plan of action for White if he wants to try to win. He should recreate the same position, perhaps after a sequence of temporizing moves with his King, but with it being Black's turn to play instead of White's. As it turns out, this can be achieved by losing a move through triangulation.

The winning procedure begins with an apparent retreat of the White King to either d4 or c4. After . . .

1. Kd4

... (or 1. Kc4, for that matter), Black should try . . .

1 ... Kd8

Or 1. Kb8, but not 1 ... Kc7 because White then plays 2. Kc5 and reaches b6 on the next move. After 1 ... Kd8, White causes Black problems with . . .

2. Kc4

(Or 2. Kd4 if the King were coming from c4 instead.) At this point, if Black instead tries . . .

2 ... Kc8

... White reestablishes the initial position by . . .

3. Kd5

But this time it is Black's turn to play. White therefore wins no matter who moves first.

Notice the White King literally outlines a triangle in its movement, going from d5 to d4 to c4 to d5 (or from d5 to c4 to d4 to d5). Also note the Black King is unable to parallel the triangulating maneuver of the White King because the pawn on c6 greatly constricts its field of operation.

Corresponding Squares

Although it's not necessary to understand the concept of corresponding squares in order to solve our problem, it might be helpful to discuss this theory from a basic point of view, for it is commonly mentioned in contemporary textbooks. Furthermore, the key maneuver used to break such correspondence is triangulation.

In pure King and pawn endgames, where pawns can't or shouldn't move, certain squares available to the White King may correspond to certain ones available to the Black. When squares are related in this way, neither side wants to be the first to occupy a corresponding square with its King. It is preferable to move to a corresponding square after the other side's King already occupies one.

Some positions contain a whole network of corresponding square-sets. A set generally consists of one corresponding square for White and one for Black. Three such sets are pertinent to our diagrammed example.

From our starting position, c5 corresponds to c7. This means White will not be able to make progress if his King occupies c5 before Black's occupies c7. It conversely means Black will lose by force if his King occupies c7 before White's does c5. In a similar way, we can say d5 for White corresponds to c8 for Black, and d6 for White corresponds to d8 for Black (stronger players will point out that it corresponds to b8 as well, but the explanation is beyond the scope of this article).

The concept can be quite elusive because corresponding squares are determined by analysis, not by formula. Each set must be ascertained by a deliberate process of investigation. This explains why books on the subject tend to provide many deeply analyzed examples and a few general statements.

An important corollary to the idea of not being the first to occupy a corresponding square is that neither side wants to move when the kings already sit on a set of corresponding squares (in our example, let's say on c5 and on c7).

Since this is the same kind of condition that underlies the concept of the opposition (that Kings stand in relation to each other and that neither one wants to move), it suggests the theories of opposition and correspondences are inextricably linked. Corresponding squares actually reflect oppositional relationships distorted by pawns of both colors.

One of the more surprising efforts on this subject was co-authored by Marcel Duchamp, the celebrated French artist. (Duchamp developed a futuristic version of Cubism, where successive phases of movement are superimposed on one another, as in multiple exposure photography.)

I was puzzled when I first learned of his book. How could an artist with such dynamic vision become so absorbed by a static aspect of chess (namely, an endgame theory dealing with fixed pawn structures)? While struggling to see the connection, it suddenly dawned on me that Duchamp had also been a guiding force behind Dada, an artistic current which tried to show that traditional logic had been rendered meaningless.

Somehow it began to make sense.

9

PLANNING AND ANALYSIS

ABCs OF CHESS—MOSCOW STYLE

Royal Heads May Have Rolled in Russia; but in the End(game), Russians Still Believe in the Power of the King

As a chess instructor, I visited the Soviet Union not merely to cover the Karpov-Kasparov match, but also to see firsthand how chess is taught in Soviet schools. It is taught very well indeed.

But everything is a "state secret" in Russia, and it was a brave and frightened young chess teacher who permitted me to attend one of his classes. The class, which was part of the regular curriculum and scheduled from nine to eleven a.m., was composed of about a dozen, mostly male, ten- and eleven-year-olds. The teaching method was Socratic: the fast tempo of question-answer and challenge-response seemed to keep the attention of the youngsters.

As for the lesson itself, it stressed the value of planning in general and the role of the King in particular. For each example, the teacher asked, "Where would you maneuver your King if given the time?" This excellent question highlighted two ideas: (1) That visualizing the future placement of pieces can be the foundation of a plan; and (2) That the King can play an active role. The first position they considered was from the famous Cohn–Rubinstein game played at St Petersburg 1909 (Diagram 1).

The teacher presented the general proposition that the more pawn groups you have, the weaker your position is. Therefore, Black's pawns, divided in two groups, were stronger than White's pawns in three groups. For our purpose, a weakness is a square on either the third or fourth rank that no pawns can protect. In the position, Black has one such weak point (d6), whereas White has several (for example, at h4 and h3).

The teacher prodded the students to show how the Black King might best exploit White's weaknesses. After a half-dozen wrong guesses, one pupil saw that a direct attack on the Kingside would give Black a commanding position. Which was exactly what happened in Cohn-Rubinstein: Black pushed his King to h3, forcing White's monarch into a passive position at g1 and h1. Rubinstein then advanced his pawns, exchanged some, and won because his better-placed King could gobble the remaining pawns.

Once again, the crux of the winning plan was the powerful endgame positioning of the Black King. The game concluded: 1 ... Kf6 2. Kd2 Kg5 3. Ke2 Kh4 4. Kf1 Kh3 5. Kg1 e5 6. Kh1 b5 7. Kg1 f5 8. Kh1 g5 9. Kg1 h5 10. Kh1 g4 11. e4 fxe4 12. fxe4 h4 13. Kg1 g3 14. hxg3 hxg3, and White resigned. It is obvious that after 15. fxg3 Kxg3 the Black King will win the e-pawn.

The teacher then introduced two positions with a related problem. In the first position, Black's pieces have virtually no scope. His

DIAGRAM 1: BLACK TO MOVE

DIAGRAM 2: WHITE WINS

Knight is actually trapped, while its White counterpart at e6 zeroes in on Black's very weak c-pawn (Diagram 2).

With Black reduced to waiting for his opponent to do something, the teacher asked, "Where should the White King go?" After some discussion, the children decided that a Queenside invasion was the most natural plan. The King would attack c7 via the route f2-e3-d4-c4-b5-a6-b7. That wins the c-pawn and the game. The teacher elucidated the plan for several minutes, whereupon he proposed a related position (Diagram 3).

As in the previous example, Black has little to do. But there are at least two differences: the White Bishop cannot attack Black's c-pawn, and Black's King at an initial glance appears able to reach the Queenside first. Here the teacher directed the class to find the best places for both of White's pieces. The pupils quickly grasped that moving the Bishop to g4 would cut off the Black King, granting the White monarch time to reach b7.

But how can White win the c-pawn? Once again, the winning plan materialized from a couple of good questions. Several students pointed out that once the White King reached b7, the Bishop could move to d7 and then exchange itself for the Knight (Bxe8). The White King would then be free to capture the crucial pawn at c7.

The teacher's final example in the lesson was from Tarrasch-Reti, played at Vienna 1922 (Diagram 4).

Although Black has more counterattacking possibilities than in the two previous positions, White enjoys a clear superiority. His more active pieces menace the Black King, and Black is also weak on the dark squares. This latter circumstance presages the correct plan.

At first, most of the kids favored capturing the e-pawn immediately with 1. Rxe6. But further analysis convinced them that the capture would dissipate White's initiative because the White Rook was more threatening on the seventh rank. To increase the pres-

DIAGRAM 3: WHITE WINS

DIAGRAM 4: WHITE TO MOVE

sure, White should bring his King into the fray. And what square could be more natural than e5? From there, it might be possible to win two pawns and to maintain most of the threats.

The teacher then played out the remainder of the game: 1. Kh2! Nd6 2. Rg7+ Kh8 (if 2 ... Kf8, then 3. Ra7+ wins) 3. Rd7! (the White Rook will now give mate should the Black Rook ever leave the back rank) 3 ... Nb5 4. Kg3 Nxc3 5. Kf4 (the advance is inexorable) 5 ... Nb5 6. Ke5 Re8 7. Kf6 Black resigned. But what is White's threat? Realizing that 8. Bg7+ would fail against 8 ... Kg8, one bright learner suggested that White's winning threat was to play 8. Kf7 and then 9. Bg7 mate. In order to stop this, Black would probably play 7 ... Kg8. The class then used about ten minutes to work out the following continuation: 8. Rg7+ Kh8 (of course not 8 ... Kf8, when 9. Rxg6 is mate) 9. Rb7 Nd6 10. Rd7 Nb5 11. Kf7 Rg8 (Black prevents 12. Bg7 mate) 12. Rd8!, and White will mate in a couple of moves.

After an hour, the class took a break. What had happened? The students surely had learned that the King can be an aggressive piece, and they now knew that in many situations its participation is crucial. Moreover, they were starting to grasp that imagining where the pieces should go is a key step in formulating a plan.

And, after all, isn't that what chess is all about—logical procedure?

ПЛОХИЕ СЛОНЫ —BAD BISHOPS

You Gotta Know When to Save 'Em—And You Gotta Know When to Trade 'Em

In the previous article, I reported on a chess lecture given in a Soviet elementary school. This article, I conclude my report on Soviet chess teaching by presenting a lesson given by IM Mark Dvoretsky, the man generally acknowledged to be the USSR's leading chess trainer. The 35-year-old Dvoretsky, who will work only with students of at least candidate master strength, has had outstanding results. Instructing no more than three or four select students a year, he has produced such formidable grandmasters as Sergei Dolmatov and Artur Yusupov.

Dvoretsky's success stems partly from the Soviet chess system, which allows him to be a full-time instructor for a mere handful of students. But only partly. For Dvoretsky differs from other Soviet trainers in the unusual range and depth of his approach. Every factor is important to him, from the psychological to the physical. With the precision of a highly trained physician, he diagnoses the least obvious flaws in a player's game. In fact, strong competitors come to him confident that he will remedy problems that they themselves cannot pinpoint.

One common obstacle Dvoretsky always tries to hurdle is pedestrian reasoning. The worst sin in this regard is superficial toadying to general chess principles. Instead he argues that chessplayers should apply objective standards when analyzing each situation. This is easier said than done for a young player on his own. So, Dvoretsky thoroughly studies a student's play, and when he detects a problem, he bombards the pupil with numerous specially designed corrective examples.

An insight into this master teacher's methods is provided by a lesson he gave on "The Bad Bishop."

A bad Bishop is one hemmed in by its own pawns. When you have such a Bishop, you generally improve its scope by placing your pawns on squares of the opposite color. And conversely, if the opponent has a bad Bishop, the rule of thumb is to fix his pawns on squares of the Bishop's color. The conventional wisdom also counsels you to trade *your* bad Bishop and to avoid trading *his*. But in this lesson Dvoretsky shows that there are exceptions to these principles.

Dvoretsky begins by quoting David Bronstein's analysis of the position shown in Diagram 1 (Taimanov-Kotov, Zurich 1953.) White, says Bronstein, has a huge advantage. His opponent has a bad Bishop, hemmed in by five of its six pawns. In addition, White's hungry Knight forces Black's minor pieces into passive defensive roles guarding c6 and g6. Nevertheless, White needs an entry into the Black camp to win. Since the a-file is controlled by Black, Bronstein offers two logical plans: (1) White can open the g-file by playing h3, Kh2, Rg1, and g4; and (2) White can advance the e-pawn by retreating the Queen, followed by f3 and e4. In both instances, the key is a pawn advance to a light square which could permit Black to trade off the pawns restricting his bad Bishop. But GM Mark

Taimanov (White) chooses neither plan. Instead, he stereotypically adheres to general principles by moving his pawns to dark squares. This fixes Black's weaknesses, but it also throws away line-opening possibilities and any real winning chances.

DIAGRAM 1: WHITE TO MOVE

DIAGRAM 2: BLACK TO MOVE

The game continued **1. h4? Kg7 2. Qg3 Qd6 3. f4? h5.** White's game looks terrific, but how does he invade the Black fortress? Dvoretsky concludes that White can no longer win with best play. But instead of answering Taimanov's **4. Be2** with 4 ... Kh7, GM Alexander Kotov (Black) went astray with **4 ... Ra4?.** He later lost after **5. Bd1 Rxb4 6. Ra1** (White captures the all-important open line) **6 ... Nc8 7. Ra8 Qe6 8. Bxh5 Kf8 9. Bxg6.**

In the following example, Black has a clear advantage (see Diagram 2, Sveshnikov-Kasparov, Minsk 1979). His King is more centralized, and his Bishop has greater scope because it is unhampered by its own pawns.

Dvoretsky suggests playing for *zugzwang* by forcing White's King to give ground or his Bishop to abandon control of e1. One suggested line is 1 ... Ba5 2. Ke2 Ke4 3. Bc5 f6 (yes, Black moves his pawn to a dark square!) 4. exf6 gxf6, and Black can follow with the plan of ... Bc7, ... Kf5 and an eventual ... e5. But Black actually played the natural **1 ... g6,** keeping White's Kingside pawns on the same color as the first player's Bishop and placing the last Black pawn on a light square. This is the normal recommended plan, but the problem with 1 ... g6 is that it leaves Black without a satisfactory breakthrough possibility. White, in fact, can probably hold now with 2. Ke2. After 2 ... Bc5 3. Be1 (the try 3. Bxc5 simplifies to a losing pawn ending) Ke4 4. Ba5, White appears to defend adequately.

Dvoretsky summarizes: "These two examples show that if your

opponent's pawns are fixed on his Bishop's color, this weakness can be exploited only by a pawn breakthrough. Therefore, you should not place all your pawns on squares opposite in color from the Bishop. Some must stay on squares of the same color to support a breakthrough."

Dvoretsky's final example illustrates that sometimes trading away your opponent's bad Bishop is better than avoiding doing so.

In Diagram 3 (Ehlvest-Andrianov, Bukhara 1981), Black should capture White's bad Bishop at e1. With this Bishop gone, White will have a harder time defending his pawns at b2 and d4.

DIAGRAM 3: BLACK TO MOVE

But Black played 1 ... **Bf8,** and the game continued **2. Bc3 a6 3. Qd2 Bc4.** Dvoretsky feels that White now has the advantage, but he must exchange away Black's bad Bishop at c4 in order to realize his chances! (It's slightly bad because the fixed d-pawn limits its scope.) A reasonable plan here might be 4. Bf1 h5 5. Bxc4 dxc4 6. Ra5 Rd5 7. Rca1, followed in good time by Qg2.

But in the game itself, White went awry. He offered to trade his bad Bishop as follows: **4. Ba5? Rdc8 5. Bb4? Bxb4 6. Qxb4 Rab8 7. Qd2.** Black has attacking possibilities along the b-file, and it seems clear that White should have kept his bad Bishop.

Dvoretsky's lesson shows that the traditional principles for playing with and against bad Bishops don't always work. The correct plan may hinge on doing just the opposite. But beyond this point, there is the general truth that even strong players tend to be inflexible.

Many of them might benefit from a few sessions with Mark Dvoretsky.

BEGINNER'S LUCK

The Novice's Boundless Enthusiasm Can Conquer Many Obstacles—Even Some That Have Baffled Pros for Ages

As a chess teacher I make a lot of general comments. Such remarks can be quite helpful and are frequently necessary. On the other hand, too much generalization can lead to shallow thinking. While this tendency can be dealt with, it's easy to see how inexperienced players may sometimes discover resources that seasoned veterans might not bother to consider. Novices have fewer preconceptions. The following example is a case in point:

WHITE TO MOVE

The above position comes from a game of Steinitz's in which he had Black. White should play 1. Ng8, since the Knight is safer when closer to the King. After 1. Ng8, the game is theoretically drawn. Instead, White played the misguided **1. Ng4?**, separating the two White pieces and leading to the loss of the Knight.

Since corralling the Knight is instructive, this example can be found throughout the literature of chess. Steinitz finished the game in what was thought to be exemplary fashion:

1. Ng4? Rh4 2. Ne3
Here 2. Nf2 loses to 2 ... Rf4 + .
2 ... Re4 3. Nd1

Other moves lose more quickly. On 3. Nf1, then 3 ... Rf4+ wins the Knight. On 3. Ng2, Black simply gathers in the Knight with his King. Finally, on 3. Nc2, the hapless piece is ensnared after 3 ... Kd5 4. Na3 Kc5 5. Nb1 Kb4 6. Nd2 Re2 7. Nb1 Rb2.

3 ... Rf4+ 4. Kg7

Here 4. Ke8 only increases the possibility of a back-rank mate.

4 ... Rf3

Reducing the Knight's scope even further.

5. Kg6 Ke5 6. Kg5 Kd4 7. Kg4

Arriving one move too late.

7 ... Rf1 8. Nb2 Rb1 9. Na4 Rb4

And the Knight is corralled.

One day I asked a student of 1150 strength to take the position home and analyze it. I didn't tell him who the players were or the result. I simply asked him to find the best continuation for Black if White plays 1. Ng4.

After burning the midnight oil, he came back the next day and wanted to know "what was wrong" with 1 ... Rh3.

As I was about to muster some instructive refutation, I noticed I couldn't. For example, 2. Ke8 allows mate in one by 2 ... Rh8. If White moves his King to the g-file, then 2 ... Rg3 pins and wins the Knight. Finally, the only safe Knight move, 2. Nf2, loses to the forking check at f3.

I was shocked.

WHITE TO MOVE

I had explained this position at least fifty times. At least two world champions had published analysis on it. But it took an 1150 player to find 1 ... Rh3. He simply did his homework.

The above example, familiar to many, is taken from the game

Cohn-Rubinstein (St. Petersburg 1909), which was analyzed earlier. Rubinstein capitalized on his superior King's position in the following manner:

1 ... g4 2. e4 fxe4 3. fxe4 h4 4. Kg1 g3 5. hxg3 hxg3, White resigns. After 6. f4, then 6 ... exf4 7. e5 g2 8. e6 Kg3 9. e7 f3, followed by 10... f2 mate.

Yet this isn't the main variation. The key line arises when White plays 2. fxg4 instead of the move he actually tried, 2. e4. No one knows what Rubinstein would have played, but Hans Kmoch and other notables have indicated that after 2 ... hxg4 3. Kg1 f4 4. exf4 exf4 5. Kh1 g3 6. fxg3 fxg3 7. hxg3 Kxg3, Black would win by virtue of getting to the Queenside pawns before White does.

For years I accepted this as the definitive treatment of the position. One day a protege of mine with a 1200 rating came to me and posed some disturbing questions. For one, in Kmoch's analysis, he wanted to know why White captures with the f-pawn instead of the h-pawn on Move 6. Not only did this violate a basic principle by capturing away from the center, but it failed to rid White of his chief problem—the weak h-pawn. So I began to look at the line 6. hxg3 fxg3 7. Kg1 (his suggestion). It seemed that after 7 ... gxf2+ 8. Kxf2, White would get to the Queenside first. It also seemed that on 7 ... g2 8. f4 Kg4 9. Kxg2 Kxf4 10. Kf2 Ke4 11. Ke2 Kd4 12. Kd2 Kc4 13. Kc2, White could hold the position even though Black has an extra tempo. Finally, the game did appear quite drawn after 7 ... Kg4 8. Kg2 gxf2 9. Kxf2. In my stupefied condition I was forced to agree with him.

So far.

Then he hit me with a real bombshell. Even if Kmoch's analysis is accepted, the final position stemming from it isn't a win anyway:

WHITE TO MOVE

The main continuation according to my student went 8. Kg1 Kf3 9. Kf1 Ke3 10. Ke1 Kd3 11. Kd1 Kc3 12. a4. Black could then win at least a pawn, but not the game. For example, 12 ... bxa4 13. Kc1 a3 14. Kb1 would lead to a book draw. Furthermore, 12 ... Kxb4 13. axb5 would also stick Black with an unpromotable Rook pawn. Finally, if Black tries to keep a Knight pawn on the board by 12 ... a6, the game would still end as a draw after 13. axb5 axb5 14. Kc1 Kxb4 15. Kb2 (thanks to the god of opposition).

As I pondered the possibility that the game had been drawn all along, my student proceeded to unveil the winning line. Apparently, Kmoch was right about not capturing toward the center, but he should have violated the principle on the second move of his analysis instead of the sixth. In other words, after 1 ... g4 2. fxg4, Black should have played 2 ... fxg4 instead of 2 ... hxg4. By capturing away from the center, Black would keep the e-pawns on the board. He would then be able to win the White e-pawn and eventually the game because of his superior King's position. Play might thereupon continue (after 2 ... fxg4): 3. Kg1 e4 (locking in the e-pawn) 4. Kh1 h4 5. Kg1 g3 6. hxg3 hxg3. Black would then win the e-pawn after 7. fxg3 Kxg3, or after 7. Kf1 gxf2 8. Kxf2 Kh2 (White gets outflanked). The thrust 7. f4 would also fail to 7 ... exf3 8. e4 g2 9. e5 Kg3, with mate next move.

I was impressed.

Right or wrong, my student had done his homework.

You may feel that the above illustrations are isolated cases, but I actually have dozens of comparable positions on file. These examples point out the surprising fallibility of the master and the hidden ability of the amateur, showing us how human both are, and how rich the game is.

10

A CONCISE BASIC COURSE IN THE CLOSED GAME

PRINCIPLES

When the Pawns Are Locked in the Center, a Game Takes on a Different Character

Thus far we have studied the principles of the open game, principles that generally apply to other kinds of positions too, with some exceptions we will note later.

A position is open if the central squares are relatively free of pawns, allowing pieces to move through the center, from one side of the board to the other. The opposite of an open game is a closed one, where pawns block the center, interfering with the piece's ability to move in the center.

CLOSED GAME

OPEN GAME

Some closed games are so different from open ones that they must develop a new set of guidelines, which we will call the Principles of the Closed Game.

Please remember that distinctions between "open" and "closed" are mainly for convenience; do not treat the following principles as absolute. Make sure they apply to the situation at hand, and even then do not use them in place of concrete analysis.

It is helpful to know how the two types of positions (open and closed) may develop. To create an open game, generally White must advance both central pawns two squares. This is easier to do if White moves his e-pawn first; the d-pawn already has support from the Queen, so it can almost always be advanced later.

For example, 1. e4 e5 2. d4 will lead to an open position if either White plays dxe5 or Black plays ... exd4. (It's not recommended that White begin a game this way; we are simply showing how easy it is to open a position by moving the e-pawn first and then the d-pawn.)

On the other hand, if White starts with 1. d4, Black can actually prevent the advance of White's e-pawn with either 1 ... d5 or 1 ... Nf6. Since White will then have to make more deliberate preparations before advancing his e-pawn, play tends to develop at a slower rate, and the position is more likely to remain closed or semiclosed.

Yet, while d-pawn openings are more likely to produce closed games, blocked centers may come about from e-pawn openings, too. For instance, a closed game can develop after the opening moves:

1. e4 e6

Black's response to White's first move is the French Defense. Black's idea is to allow White to establish a pawn center, and then to strike back by 2 ... d5; we will discuss the strengths and weaknesses of this plan as the game continues:

2. d4

This move makes a lot of sense. After 2. d4, White seizes space and temporary control of the center. He can also develop all his pieces without having to move another pawn (the main reason being that he can develop both of his Bishops easily). In fact, for development's sake, it's usually best to advance these two pawns in most openings, open or closed. But since this is generally easier to do in e-pawn openings, we offer this final open game principle:

• Try to Advance Both Center Pawns Two Squares Each

Our game continued:
2 ... d5
In response to the attack against his e-pawn, White has three basic choices: (1) he can advance his e-pawn; (2) he can exchange pawns; or (3) he can defend his e-pawn. Let's examine these options in detail.

(1) *He plays 3. e5:* This move would "lock" the center, creating a closed game (notice how the pawn structure would resemble the example of a closed game we showed you earlier). For practical reasons, we say the pawn chain consists only of pawns that are locked into place. Thus, White's portion of the chain is made up of the pawns at d4 and e5, while Black's chain consists of the pawns at d5 and e6 (but not the pawn at f7, which is still free to move).

Furthermore, the base of White's chain is at d4, and the base of Black's is at e6. According to Aron Nimzovich, a brilliant chess thinker and player of the early 20th century, the chain should be attacked at its base; if the base is undermined, the whole thing might topple.

If White has the chance, he will advance a pawn to f5, trying to undermine e6; Black will play ... c5 to attack d4. Clearly, Black has a much better chance of carrying out his plan than White. In fact, White may never be able to play f5. Therefore, while White gets an advantage in space after 3. e5, Black seize the initiative with the

POSITION AFTER 2 ... d5

sharp countermove 3 ... c5. So, we have our first closed game principle (which is slightly less true for open games):

- Closed Game Principle #1:
  To Gain Space, You Usually Have to Sacrifice Time

Notice that Black's pawns block his light-squared Bishop, which in the French Defense is often called the "problem Bishop." Since it is limited in scope, especially when compared to White's light-squared counterpart, Black tried to exchange it for just about any of White's minor pieces. Thus, you can see that closed games are better suited to Knights than Bishops, though this is by no means always the case:

- Closed Game Principle #2:
  Knights Can Sometimes Be Better Than Bishops

(2) *He can exchange pawns:* After 3. exd5 exd5, White's advantage would truly be reduced to having the first move. The exchange not only ends the tension in the center, it also solves the problem of Black's bad Bishop—to Black's advantage. While symmetrical positions almost always favor White, sometimes, as in this case, the advantage is small. Exchanging is probably best if White is merely playing for a draw.

3. *He can defend his e-pawn:* This is what White decided to do, but there are several ways to do the job. We leave you to consider this until next time. Consider which defenses are plausible, and why. Furthermore, decide what is wrong with the protective move 3. f3. On the surface, doesn't it keep White's pawn center intact? Give it some thought, and check the answer in the next article.

POSITIONAL SENSE

In a Closed Game, Factors Like Piece Placement and Development of a Plan Are Vital to Success

The moves of our game so far: **1. e4 e6 2. d4 d5.** We ended the last section by asking you to evaluate reasonable defenses for White's e-pawn and, in particular, if there was anything wrong with the protective move 3. f3.

The answer is that 3. f3 drops a pawn after 3 ... dxe4 4. fxe4 Qh4 +. It also gives Black a crushing attack.

POSITION AFTER 2 ...d5

Other defenses are more promising. The move 3. Bd3 is safer, but it loses the initiative to 3 ... dxe4 4. Bxe4 Nf6. It also violates an Open Game Principle (develop Knights before Bishops), still in force here as the game has not yet become closed.

Another idea is to play 3. Nd2, steering the game into quieter waters and allowing White to aim for a slight but lasting advantage. Note that 3. Nd2 also avoids the pesky Winawer Variation (3. Nc3 Bb4), because then the attempted Bishop pin of 3 ... Bb4 would run smack into 4. c3. World Champion Anatoly Karpov prefers 3. Nd2, using it in numerous encounters with Viktor Korchnoi. In a typical variation, White plays to isolate Black's d-pawn: 3 ... c5 4. exd5 exd5

5. Nf3 Nc6 6. Bb5 Bd6 7. dxc5. Instead of this popular continuation, White played the equally good:

3. Nc3

This allows the sharp 3 ... Bb4, which indirectly threatens the e-pawn. (The Knight which protects it would be pinned and perhaps captured later.) On the other hand, 3. Nc3 gives White greater attacking chances than 3. Nd2. Instead of the Winawer, which usually commits Black to exchanging his dark-squared Bishop for White's Knight on c3, Black chose a more classical response.

3 ... Nf6

This maintains the tension in the center, forcing White to do something about his e-pawn. Probably the best, and certainly the sharpest, continuation is 4. Bg5. The pin keeps the pressure on Black and threatens the advance 5. e5, which brings to mind an Open Game Principle (try to attack pinned pieces, especially with pawns). Black would have several ways to deal with that possibility, such as breaking the pin with 4 ... Be7 or even exchanging pawns on e4. Instead, White decides to take a stand and fixes the center at once:

4. e5

Now we have a closed game; the central pawn chain blocks movement through the middle of the board, slowing play considerably. Attention will now shift to the pawn chain itself, and the play around it. Black will attempt to undermine the chain while White will try to uphold it. Black will especially focus on the pawn at e5, which cramps his position. He must also worry about finding a good post for his light-squared Bishop. Will Black be able to increase its scope, or exchange it for another minor piece?

4 ... Nfd7

White must prepare for the attack against his center. He can reposition his Queen's Knight to e2, for example, which would prepare to answer 5 ... c5 with 6. c3. This would allow White the chance to maintain his pawn chain. Or, he could forego the chain altogether and protect his e-pawn directly. In that case, he would still be able to keep Black's "problem Bishop" hemmed in. Both ideas are reasonable, but White chose the latter.

5. f4 c5

A good try now for White is the straightforward 6. Nf3. Beyond the fact that it develops a piece, it might entice Black into erroneously locking the game with 6 ... c4, a move that superficially hampers White's light-squared Bishop. But, in fact, Black's light-squared counterpart would suffer the most after this premature push. At least White's Bishop could still be useful on the Kingside. It might even be able to help in an attack against the pawn at c4. Meanwhile, Black's problem Bishop would be useless, completely trapped behind a wall of its own pawns. This suggests a corollary to an Open Game Principle (advance your pawns onto the opposite color of your Bishop):

- Closed Game Principle #3:
Don't Block in Your Bishops
With Pawns

The move 6 ... c4 in this possible variation is bad also because it's inconsistent. Black plays 5 ... c5 to attack the center, not to lock it. It's important to be flexible, to be able to adjust to shifting fortunes, but you shouldn't jump from one idea to another aimlessly. You shouldn't change a plan without a solid reason. If you try to do too many things, you'll wind up doing nothing:

- Closed Game Principle #4:
Choose a Plan and Stay With It—
Change It Only If You Should or Must

6. dxc5
Black may continue in several ways. He could develop his Knight to c6, postponing the immediate recapture of the pawn (it can't run away). Or, he could take back at once with his Knight on d7, which would provide central play and speed up the problem Bishop's development. Or . . .
6 ... Bxc5
From c5, the Bishop cuts across the center, preventing White from Kingside castling (although White can eventually counter this). For now, we leave you with a question. Black's dark-squared Bishop is powerful, but does it actually threaten anything? Turn to the next article for the answer.

POSITION AFTER 6 ... Bxc5

BE SNEAKY

When the Position Is Unclear, It Pays to Be a Master of Deception

Six moves have been played so far: **1. e4 e6 2. d4 d5 3. Nc3 Nf6 4. e5 Nfd7 5. f4 c5 6. dxc5 Bxc5**

Last month we ended by asking if Black's dark-squared Bishop, though menacingly poised, actually threatens anything. If given the chance, Black would certainly take White's Knight at g1. This would force White to recapture with his Rook, thus losing his right to castle Kingside. This suggests a corollary to an Open Game Principle (castle early)—namely, *try to prevent your opponent from castling.*

POSITION AFTER 6 ... Bxc5

But, beyond losing the right to castle, White would lose a pawn. After taking back on g1, White would see his h-pawn fall to a forking Queen check by Black at h4. Thus we have an addition to another Open Game Principle #9 (develop with threats): *Look for double attacks.* White's next move averts both disasters:

7. Nf3

A good continuation for Black would be 7 ... Nc6; after 8. Bd3, he could try to undermine White's e-pawn by 8 ... f6. This plan makes sense if Black wants to free his position, which is severely cramped by the pawn at e5. The idea works as long as White can't exploit the weakening of the e8-h5 and d3-h7 diagonals. One of Black's main concerns must be improving the condition of his light-squared Bishop; this situation might be helped by a few exchanges. Which leads us to:

- Closed Game Principle #5:
If Cramped, Free Your Game
by Exchanges

7 ... a6
This prepares the advance of the b-pawn, but it also places another pawn on a light square. That makes it harder for Black to improve the scope of his problem Bishop (the one at c8) because it travels only in light squares.

8. Bd3
Note how good a post this is for White's light-squared Bishop. When you compare it to its Black counterpart, you can appreciate the magnitude of Black's difficulties. If Black could trade his obstructed Bishop, he would improve his chances greatly. Therefore:

- Closed Game Principle #6: Trade Bad Minor Pieces for Good Ones

8 ... Nc6 9. Qe2
This is a useful waiting move. In some variations, it makes possible the offer of a Bishop exchange on e3, which would restore White's right to castle Kingside. (Note, however, an immediate 10. Be3 would lose a piece to the forking advance 10 ... d4.) Moreover, with the Queen at e2, Black may think twice about breaking with the pawn move f6, because opening the e-file might prove troublesome (Black's exposed e-pawn would be vulnerable). Finally, though it is not currently in the cards, 9. Qe2 speeds the opportunity of Queenside castling. Overall, 9. Qe2 retains most plans, without giving away White's intentions. It also implies:

- Closed Game Principle #7:
If the Position is Unsettled, Disguise Your Plans; Make Noncommittal Moves

9 ... Nb4?
This may seem a good idea because it gets rid of White's light-squared Bishop. On the other hand, the position might easily become more closed and suited to Knights. Thus, Black's action is premature and too committal. If he trades a minor piece, it should be his problem Bishop. That's going to be harder to do once White's light-squared Bishop is gone. Black's Knight sortie, therefore, betrays his confusion.

10. Bd2

White chooses a sound, cautious scheme of development—he waits for Black to hang himself. There's a lot more bite to this move, however, than is immediately obvious.

10 ... b5

Although Black's advance seems aggressive, it has the drawback of placing another pawn on a light square. Perhaps he thought he could post his problem Bishop at b7, but that wouldn't necessarily improve its condition either, as we shall soon see.

11. Nd1

This is a repositioning, not a retreat. It also presents a minor threat—namely, to trade White's slightly bad Bishop (his dark-squared one) for Black's Knight, thus preserving his better Bishop at d3. Why is White's dark-squared Bishop slightly bad? Because some of White's pawns are fixed on squares of the same color. Black's problem Bishop is also blocked by its own pawns, but its difficulties are worse because Black has less space. (Generally, the further you advance your pawns, the more space you get behind the lines.) Thus we can deduce:

• Closed Game Principle #8:
To Gain Space Advance Key Pawns

11 ... Nxd3 + 12. cxd3!

This is better than taking back with the Queen, because now White gets an open c-file for his Rooks. Open lines are particularly useful in closed positions, where there tend to be few roads into the enemy's camp. Thus we have:

• Closed Game Principle #9:
Seize Open Lines

12 ... Qb6

A mistake. While trying to increase his hold on the a7-g1 diagonal,

Black blindly cuts off his dark-squared Bishop's line of retreat. It would be a tragedy for Black if this Bishop—his best-placed piece—were driven from its fine post. Instead, he should have played 12 ... b4, which would have prevented what follows.

13. b4!

The turning point, so to speak. Black's powerful Bishop is forced back. Staying on the a7-g1 diagonal would now prove disastrous. For example, after 13 ... Bd4, White would win a piece after 14. Rb1 (protecting the b-pawn). The problem is that White is going to play Nxd4 next; and if Black takes back with his Queen, he loses it to Be3 (note the significance of Rb1).

13 ... Be7

POSITION AFTER 13 ... Be7

As we leave you this time, consider the natural follow-up to White's last move. Shouldn't he try to drive Black's Queen off the same a7-g1 diagonal? Why not 14. Be3 at once, attacking the Queen? See the next article for the answer.

SLOW BUT SURE

Be Patient. In Closed Games, Haste Makes Waste

Thirteen moves have been played so far: **1. e4 e6 2. d4 d5 3. Nc3 Nf6 4. e5 Nfd7 5. f4 c5 6. dxc5 Bxc5 7. Nf3 a6 8. Bd3 Nc6 9. Qe2 Nb4 10. Bd2 b5 11. Nd1 Nxd3+ 12. cxd3 Qb6 13. b4 Be7**

We concluded the last article by asking if White should play 14. Be3. Although he does want to drive Black's Queen off the a7-g1 diagonal, White can't play 14. Be3 because of 14 ... Bxb4+. This *zwischenzug* (or in-between move) by Black wins a pawn because White is forced to get out of check first. On the next move (or after 15. Bd2 Bxd2+), Black can move his Queen to safety.

POSITION AFTER 13 ... Be7

14. a3
Black should now concentrate on freeing his cramped position. One idea is 14 ... d4, preventing Be3 and opening the a8-f3 diagonal for Black's problem Bishop. If White continues with 15. Qe4 (remember to look for double attacks), then 15 ... Bb7 16. Qxd4 Bxf3 17. Qxb6 Nxb6 18. gxf3 Nd5 19. a3 Rc8 seems to give Black more than enough for his sacrificed pawn. Another promising possibility is 14 ... f6, attempting to free his game.
14 ... f5?
This push makes no sense. Black should try to improve the scope of his light-squared Bishop, not worsen it. By playing f5 instead of f6, Black violates two Closed Game Principles: #3 (don't block your Bishops with pawns) and #5 (if cramped, free your game by exchanging pieces).
15. Rc1
Since there's no need to play Be3 immediately, White grabs the open c-file, in accordance with Closed Game Principle #9 (seize open lines).
15 ... Bb7
One must wonder about this Bishop's future. Note that 15 ... d4 would open the long diagonal but lose a pawn after 16. Qf2.
16. Be3 Qd8
Black's last move was forced. By driving the Black Queen back, White takes control of another open line: the a7-g1 diagonal.
17. Nd4
What a post for a Knight! From d4 it overlooks key squares, placing real pressure on Black's game. We now see why a closed position may be better suited to Knights than Bishops. The fixed

pawns do not hinder White's Knight—it can jump over the central barrier. On the other hand, Black's Bishop at b7 is literally walled in. Notice how the Knight both attacks and blockades, putting pressure on Black and preventing him from making a freeing advance with his d-pawn.

17 ... Nf8

Black had to protect his e-pawn. A mistake would have been 17 ... Qb6 because of 18. Nxf5, with a discovered attack on the Queen.

18. 0-0

This late castling illustrates an important difference between open and closed positions. You usually castle early in open positions because an open center often puts your King in danger. With the center locked, however, the King is safer. In some closed games it's best to leave your King in the center until you can tell if pawn advances will open up one flank or the other.

White has resisted playing d3-d4, which novices might like because it makes a "prettier" pawn structure. But it has serious drawbacks. First, it makes White's dark-squared Bishop a problem Bishop, robbing it of scope. Second, Black might gain counterplay by transferring a Knight to c4. Finally, in these types of positions d4 is best for a piece. For example, in the middlegame it makes an excellent post for a Knight, while a King is often well-placed there in the endgame.

- Closed Game Principle #10:
  If the Center Is Blocked, Don't Automatically Castle

18 ... h5

Perhaps Black was afraid of 19.g4, because if he plays 19 ... fxg4, then 20. f5 will open up the game in White's favor. Black isn't ready for a fight since his pieces lag in development. This suggests:

- Closed Game Principle #11:
  If Behind in Development, Keep the Game Closed

Black's last move puts yet another pawn on a light square, making life miserable for his light-squared Bishop. But then, it's hard to find good moves here.

19. Nc3

Let's take stock. White has an advantage in:
- *space*, because his pawns are more advanced and his pieces have greater mobility;
- *time*, because he's better developed and has the initiative;

• *King safety,* though this is not yet significant with the position closed; and

• *pawn structure,* because he has fewer weaknesses and his pawns help his pieces, whereas Black's pawns block his own forces.

Individually, these fine points seem unimportant, but collectively they are overwhelming. Clearly, White has the upper hand. So far, Black has not had to give up material to counter these "small advantages," but he may have to eventually. Since small advantages can be important, especially when grouped together, we have:

• Closed Game Principle #12:
Try to Accumulate Small Advantages

White's last move started a maneuver. Because this Knight was the least developed of all his pieces, he has decided to make greater use of it. Try to guess where the Knight is headed.

19 ... Kf7
This is played to relieve the Knight at f8, which has been tied down defending e6. It reveals Black's limited number of options.

20. Nb1!
Where is the Knight going?

20 ... g6
We don't mean to sound like a broken record, but Black seems oblivious to the problem of his light-squared Bishop. With all his pawns now fixed on light squares, he must be careful not to exchange his King's Bishop. Otherwise, the dark squares would be indefensible. Black avoided 20 ... Nd7 because 21. Nxf5 exf5 22. e6 + Kf8 (but not 22 ... Kxe6 23. Bb6 +, winning the Queen) opens up the game for White's better developed pieces (though the resulting position is unclear).

POSITION AFTER 23. Na5

21. Nd2 Nd7 22. N2b3
Finally, it appears White's Knight is headed for c5. White has had the time for this maneuver because the position has been closed.
22 ... Rc8
Black plays this to fight for control of the c-file. The Rook also attacks the square c5, which may be White's goal.
23. Na5
Although this move attacks the Bishop on b7, it appears to contradict an Open Game Principle (a Knight on the rim is grim). It is true that in open positions Knights have less mobility on the edge of the board. But this is a closed position, where a slightly different set of principles applies.

For next time, try to think of reasons for the Knight's placement at a5. Is it a good or bad post? Support your evaluation with concrete reasons. Next article: the explanation.

THE KILL

The Wolf, Circling for a While, Is Ready for the Final Assault

The preceding moves of our game were: **1. e4 e6 2. d4 d5 3. Nc3 Nf6 4. e5 Nfd7 5. f4 c5 6. dxc5 Bxc5 7. Nf3 a6 8. Bd3 Nc6 9. Qe2 Nb4 10. Bd2 b5 11. Nd1 Nxd3+ 12. cxd3 Qb6 13. b4 Be7 14. a3 f5 15. Rc1 Bb7 16. Be3 Qd8 17. Nd4 Nf8 18. 0-0 h5 19. Nc3 Kf7 20. Nb1 g6 21. Nd2 Nd7 22. Nb3 Rc8 23. Na5**

When we left you last time, we asked about the Knight's effectiveness at a5. In open games, Knights are generally most effective in the center. Sometimes, as in our game, the wing can provide a fine base for a Knight, especially if it has a safe post and nearby targets to attack. At a5, the Knight hits the bishop at b7; it also threatens, when the time is right, to invade c6. We must conclude that the Knight at a5 is safe from harm and ready for action.

POSITION AFTER 23. Na5

23 ... Ba8 24. Rxc8
The premature 24. Nc6 allows Black to exchange his light-squared Bishop. By trading Rooks, White seizes the c-file, the main highway into the opposing camp.
24 ... Qxc8 25. Rc1 Qb8
Black hopes to fight for the c-file with 26 ... Rc8. Can White stop this?
26. Qc2!
Some of the best moves are the simplest.

• Closed Game Principle # 13:
To Strengthen Control of a File,
Double Your Major Pieces
(Rooks and/or Queen) on It

Now that White can use the c-file as an avenue of attack, attention should shift to the square c7 and, more generally, to the seventh rank. Rooks and Queens can wield enormous power along this rank, often attacking a whole line of pawns and pieces. On the seventh, major pieces can also pester advancing pawns by getting behind them. And by occupying the seventh rank, attacking pieces can sometimes launch direct assaults against the opposing King. Thus:

• Closed Game Principle #14:
Try to Dominate the Seventh Rank

26 ... Bd8
Black tries to prevent 27. Qc7.
27. Nac6!
After 27 ... Bxc6, White retakes with his Queen, simultaneously attacking a6, e6, and d7.
27 ... Qb7 28. Nxd8 + Rxd8 29. Qc7

White wastes no time exploiting the weakened dark squares now that Black's good Bishop is gone. This intrusion on the seventh rank may seem of little consequence. But positional play is based on accumulating such small advantages.

29 ... Qb8

This protects the Rook. Trading Queens instead would have only brought White's Rook menacingly to the seventh. By keeping his Queen, Black has at least some chance to defend his vulnerable Queenside.

Black remains cramped and under attack, but it isn't clear how White's attack should proceed. Should he head for an ending by trading Queens? Should he try to improve his game further. If so, how?

Consider the first idea, exchanging Queens. After 31. Qxb8 Rxb8, for example, a direct invasion (say, 32. Rc7 Rb7 33. Rc6 Rb6 34. Rc8 Rb8) doesn't accomplish much.

So we turn to the second question: can White improve his game? In effect, we're asking if White's pieces are placed as strongly as they could be. One should be doing more. White's Bishop has great potential now that Black's dark-squared Bishop is gone. But does it have targets? A Black piece is tied to a dark square—the Rook at d8, which must protect the pinned Knight at d7. How can White exploit this?

30. Bf2!

The threat is 31. Bh4, and Black's bad pawn play has left him helpless to stop it. If you discovered this move through careful, structured reasoning, you used a technique known to all accomplished chessplayers:

- Closed Game Principle #15:
  Use the Analytic Method:
  Evaluate, Then Question

The analytic method is especially applicable when you don't know what to do. First step: ask questions. Who stands better, and why? What is the threat? Do you have threats? Can you improve your position?

It's not always easy to ask the right questions, and it's harder still to find the right answers. As a beginner, you'll likely make mistakes (even grandmasters do). But, even if you're wrong, this approach is better than random thinking.

30 ... Qb6 31. Nf3
Practically forcing a trade.
31 ... Qxc7 32. Rxc7 Ke8
To free the Rook.
33. Ng5 Nf8
Not 33 ... Ke7 34. Bc5 +.
34. Bc5
Threatening 35. Re7 mate, and 35. Bxf8.
34 ... Nd7

POSITION AFTER BLACK RESIGNED

White can now safely play 35. Nxe6. Since the pawn can't run away, however, White decides to keep his good Bishop and tighten the noose.

35 Bd6, Black resigns!

Let's evaluate. Black's e-pawn is threatened, and he can't defend it (35 ... Nf8 allows, among other things, 36. Re7 mate). The King doesn't have a legal move, and the Bishop doesn't have a safe one. Black can shift his Rook to b8, but then 36. Rxd7 wins a piece (36 ... Kxd7 37. Bxb8). That leaves the Knight. If 35 ... Nb6, for example, then 36. Re7 + Kf8 37. Nh7 + (yes, 37. Nxe6 + also wins) 37 ... Kg8 38. Nf6 + Kf8 (or 38 ... Kh8 39. Rh7, mate) 39. Rd7 is mate. Reduced to a couple of harmless pawn moves, unable to defend e6, Black resigned—without having yet lost a single thing!

This 1885 game was played in Baltimore between World Champion Wilhelm Steinitz (White) and A. G. Selman (Black).

White realized the game was closed, and he knew what to do. He was content to control open lines, avoid weaknesses and premature commitments, develop pieces and pawns harmoniously, and so on. He understood that, by accumulating these small advantages, he could build an overwhelming position—and then win.

INDEX

About the Author

Bruce Pandolfini, a U.S. National Chess Master, gained prominence as an analyst on PBS's live telecast of the Fischer-Spassky championship match in 1972. In due course, he lectured widely on chess and in 1978 was chosen to deliver the Bobby Fischer Chess Lectures at the University of Alabama in Birmingham. He is the author of *Let's Play Chess, Bobby Fischer's Outrageous Chess Moves, One Move Chess by the Champions,* and *Principles of the New Chess.* He is also a *Chess Life* magazine consulting editor, for which he writes the monthly "ABCs of Chess," and he has written columns for *Time-Video,* the *Litchfield County Times,* and *Physician's Travel and Meeting Guide.*

As a chess teacher, he's been on the faculty of the New School for Social Research since 1973, and currently conducts chess classes at Browning, Trinity, and the Little Red School House in New York City. With U.S. Champion Lev Alburt, he has developed special children's programs sponsored by the American Chess Foundation. The director of the world famous Manhattan Chess Club at Carnegie Hall, Pandolfini visited the USSR in the fall of 1984 to study their teaching methods and observe the controversial championship match between Anatoly Karpov and Gary Kasparov.